Getting Clients

For Lawyers Starting Out or Starting Over

MERRILYN ASTIN TARLTON

Thank you, Steve для your thoughtful suggestions!

Merrilyn Astin Tarlton

12.8.2016

ONE REALLY GOOD IDEA EVERY DAY
attorneyatwork@

© 2016 by Merrilyn Astin Tarlton

All rights reserved. No part of this book may be reproduced or transmitted in any form by any means, electronic or mechanical, including photocopying, recording or by information storage and retrieval system, without permission from the publisher.

Published by Attorney at Work, USA.

Design by Feldcomm.

Illustrations © iStockPhoto.com/elenabs

ISBN: 978-0-9895293-6-5

ONE REALLY GOOD IDEA EVERY DAY
attorneyatwork@™

www.attorneyatwork.com

*This book is dedicated to the wisest men
I know, Steve and Jesse.*

Contents

Acknowledgments — vii
About the Author — ix

Introduction: This Is Your Job — 1

Gathering the Raw Materials — 5

Part 1: Pointing in the Right Direction — 10
Focus in on your mission, market and product.

1. What Do You Want to Do With Your Life? — 13
   Fill in the Blanks — 14
2. Product Development — 17
   Checklist: Getting Ready to Go to Market — 20
3. Who Buys What You Have to Sell? — 23
   The Exercise — 24

Part 2: Exploring the Marketing Menu — 28
Select the best tactics for your personal marketing plan.

4. The Star-Maker Machinery — 31
5. You, Online — 35
6. Your Website — 39
7. Content Marketing — 43
8. Tips for Making More Impact With Your Content — 51
9. Marketing Materials — 57

10. Joining the Right Organization	61
Convene Your Own Club	66
11. Finding the Right Speaking Engagements	69
12. Leave Them Speechless When You Give a Speech	73
13. Advertising and Publicity	79

Part 3: Networking and Personal Sales — 82

Get ready to put your unique self out there.

14. Networking	85
15. That Elevator Speech	91
16. Proposals: Give Them Something to Say Yes To	95
17. Pitches and Presentations	99
18. Laying the Groundwork for Referrals	103
19. Cross-Selling	107

The Marketing Emergency — 111

Part 4: Getting It Done — 114

Solidify your plan and stay motivated.

20. Your Marketing Plan Worksheet	117
21. Project Managing Your Marketing Plan	123
Getting Really Creative	128
22. Keeping Track of Your Progress	131
23. Staying Motivated	135
24. Steer Clear of These Potholes	139
Don't Forget	143

Acknowledgments

I began working with lawyers in 1984, a mere seven years after *Bates v. State Bar of Arizona* changed everything. While I arrived at my first big law firm with a decade of marketing experience, the lawyers and I had to learn together how to apply marketing theory to a centuries-old profession that had long been secure in the belief that lawyers must *never* actively publicize their services.

It is those lawyers, and the many hundreds who succeeded them, I must acknowledge for their contributions—large and small—to the body of knowledge this book represents.

Often, a lawyer has asked me to recommend a book with instructions for getting clients. While there are many wonderful books about marketing legal services for firms, I was never able to find the book that spoke to a single lawyer, alone in the need to find and get clients. What was needed was an answer to the perennial plea, "Tell me what to do!"

It is my hope that *this* is that book.

There are specific people who must be thanked. W. Harold "Sonny" Flowers, Jr., the lawyer who first opened my eyes to the difference between marketing a firm and marketing a lawyer. William C. McClearn, the lawyer who showed me that the highest level of professionalism can be one and the same as effective business development. Bob Denney, who wrote "How to Market Legal Services" almost before it was an actual thing. Bruce W. Marcus, a pioneer in accounting firm marketing, who shined a clear light on the way forward for the legal profession.

Thanks must especially be given to Jordan Furlong for extraordinary collegiality, inspiration, advice and support in the writing of this book. To my friends Mary Beth Pratt, Simon Chester, Vedia Jones-Richardson, Heidi Alexander, Steve Nelson, Marian Lee and Tim Henderson for their expert review and notes. I owe a debt of gratitude to Joy White for her always impeccable edits and most of all to my partners, Joan Feldman and Mark Feldman, for believing that I could.

About the Author

Merrilyn Astin Tarlton has been helping lawyers think differently about the practice of law since 1984 when she became one of North America's first law firm marketing executives. Today, she works with individuals and organizations to redefine success in the new business of law.

Merrilyn is a founding member and past president of the Legal Marketing Association and a past president and trustee of the College of Law Practice Management. She was honored to be inducted into the inaugural class of the LMA Hall of Fame (also known as the Lifetime Achievement Award) and as a Fellow in the College.

A former editor-in-chief of the American Bar Association's magazine, Law Practice, Merrilyn was the first chair of the ABA's Beyond the Breaking Point Task Force, and has been published hundreds of times in electronic and print publications. Much of her recent work has focused on trends impacting the future of the profession and creating and managing change in law firms. In 2010, she launched Attorney at Work with partners Joan Feldman and Mark Feldman.

She lives in Golden, Colorado, with her husband, Steve, and their cats, Margaret Elizabeth and Agnes Jane.

Follow Merrilyn at Attorneyatwork.com and Getting-clients.com and on Twitter @AstinTarlton.

Introduction: This Is Your Job

I was once called to an employment lawyer's office and asked to explain exactly what I could do for him—I was the firm's new marketing director. "Well," I said, "what would you like me to do?"

Exuding an icy charm, this guy (let's call him John) tipped his chair back, crossed his ankles on the desk and began: "I'd like you to call me on the phone one afternoon a few weeks from now and ask me to come to the 35th-floor conference room where you will have convened a group of eight general counsel from Fortune 500 companies. Each will have a complex wrongful termination situation with which they need immediate legal help, and you will have determined ahead of time that none of them present conflict issues for me, the firm or with each other. Can you do that?"

He was serious.

I think the desired response was, "Yes, sir!" What I actually said was, "I can't do that for you, John. But let's talk about how you can do that for yourself."

And that is what this book is about.

It's Up to You

There are lots of books about business development for lawyers out there. But this one is different. It will not only help you focus and make ongoing sense of your marketing activities, it will also lead to getting the type of clients you want and building the sustainable law practice you dream of. No more throwing mud at the wall to see what sticks! By working through the steps in this book in order, you'll know exactly what you want and how to go about getting it, with a tight list of criteria for assessing your marketing options.

Sure, I could give you a little list of things to do to bring in a few clients. You could hop right on it and end up with enough general work to keep you busy doing something for a couple of weeks.

Or we could start with the end in mind, identify the precise kind of work you want to do and then get busy bringing in clients who want that kind of help—a more productive, cost-effective, satisfying and long-term approach.

"Getting Clients: For Lawyers Just Starting Out or Starting Over" takes the latter approach. If at first it feels a little inside out to you, just hang in there.

This is going to be good.

7 STEPS TO GETTING CLIENTS

GET CLIENTS →

1. Gather raw materials
2. Figure out the kind of work
3. Focus in on the kinds of clients
4. Figure out what your market needs
5. Explore possible marketing tactics
6. Pursue networking and personal sales
7. Execute your personal marketing plan

" No more throwing mud at the wall to see what sticks!"

Gathering the Raw Materials

You are already in possession of some important elements of your personal marketing plan and you'll want to make sure you've got them all in one place.

Regardless of how you focus your practice, you need to gather together these two sets of information:

- Everyone you know

- Everything there is to know about the professional you

In both instances, these will be databases that should follow you throughout your career. You'll constantly add to and refine them, keeping the information current.

If you are considering leaving an existing practice and have this information scattered across the firm's systems and other places, now is a good time to pull all this data into your own files before it is left irretrievably behind. If you're a brand-spanking new lawyer, you get the advantage of building a good foundation for both of these information sets right from the get-go. Later, you're more likely to put it off because you're too busy, and then you'll lose important marketing ground. So, here's how it works.

Your Collected Contacts

Wherever you are in your career, you have groups of friends, colleagues, family members and others—information about whom you'll want to preserve in *one place* for easier retrieval later, if you haven't already. Open a new spreadsheet and create the following column headings across the top. (We're using a spreadsheet format so you'll be able to easily convert to any contact management app you use.)

- Last Name
- First Name
- Organization
- Street Address 1
- Street Address 2
- City
- State/Province
- Zip/Postal Code
- Country
- Email Address
- Phone
- Website URL
- Notes

Now gather up those stray business cards, directories and rosters and start dropping the information into those spreadsheet blanks horizontally. You'll want a record of all kinds of contacts:

- Teachers
- Neighbors
- College and law school classmates
- Roommates
- Professors
- Sponsors
- Former partners
- Fellow interns
- Committee members

It will look something like this:

LAST NAME	FIRST NAME	ORGANIZATION	ADDRESS 1	ADDRESS 2	CITY	STATE	ZIP CODE	EMAIL	PHONE #	URL	NOTES
Grainger	Stewart	Flix. Inc.	555 17th St.	Suite 7400	Boulder	CO	80301	s.grain@flixit.com	720.999.8100	www.flixit.com	College roommate
Banks	Brenda	Verve	123 Crossbars Ave.		Silicon	ID	90001	brendab@verve.com	555.620.3777	www.verve.com	Board President, Hearthside Helpers
Anderson	Roger	ILMPCO	3700 Highway 5	Suite 100	Des Moines	IA	50311	roger.anders@ilmpco.net	801.222.1801	www.ilmpco.net	
Franklin-Guest	Rita		663 Black Dahlia St.		Mapleton	WI	40333	r.guest@yahoo.com	440.921.4545		PR Consultant
Phillips	Reagan	Practical Fact	21 S. Woodrush St.	Suite 650	Spokane	WA	99201	r.phillips@practfact.com	201.150.0978	www.practfact.com	

Include *anyone* you may want to keep in touch with going forward—professionally or socially. You'll be surprised how many there are. Resist the urge to cull any at this point. You never know who might be

THE RAW MATERIALS 7

important five years from now. And if you wait until later to back up and track someone down, it may not be so easy to find them.

If you can't find the time to do this yourself, get your assistant, a high-schooler or a temp to do it. Trust me, it's worth it, even if you have to pay a bit to get the data entered.

Your Resume Database

Of course, you've written a resume before. But it was probably refined and tailored to the specific purpose. The document you'll be assembling here is going to be all-inclusive.

Start from scratch and be completely comprehensive. Include everything from the titles of papers you wrote, to law school addresses, to special projects and advisers' names. Make certain you include the name of that presentation you made, and the venue where you made it. Record positive written feedback you have received from clients, audience members and others, including the name and organization of each person who gave it to you and the date. (That person's information is included in your contact list as well, right?)

Don't worry if it seems like too much information. It is. But you'll never use it in this format. This document's purpose is to serve as a master database from which all future resumes, biographies or curriculum vitae will be drawn.

I promise you'll be glad you did the groundwork up-front.

Now that you've taken care of those, set them aside and let's begin.

THE LAWYER WHO GETS CLIENTS

Of course, there is more to getting (and keeping) good clients than marketing, networking, elevator speeches and the rest. Clients will assume a number of additional things about you. The successful lawyer is a well-rounded businessperson *and* an effective lawyer. How do you stack up?

The lawyer who gets clients ...

- ☐ Is a good, smart and effective lawyer, constantly learning and building new skills to help clients solve their legal problems.
- ☐ Accepts the responsibility to know and conform to the ethical and legal requirements of her practice.
- ☐ Takes personal responsibility for building his own practice, regardless of the size, setting or location of his firm.
- ☐ Knows that fees based solely on how long it takes to do the work are a thing of the past, and instead extends fees reflecting the work's value to the client.
- ☐ Commits to be smart about the application of evolving technologies to better meet clients' needs.

PART 1
Pointing in the Right Direction

There are so many different tools lawyers can use to promote their services—advertising, networking, blogging, public speaking ... it can quickly get pretty overwhelming. So, as with any other voyage worth taking, it's important to first figure out where you really want to go. Then, armed with that information, you can begin to identify the best steps to get you there.

In this segment, you will:

1. Identify your **personal mission**—the kind of work you want to do.

2. Figure out your **target market**—who you want to do that work for and who, specifically, will likely pay you to do it.

3. Flesh out your **product**—gather and assemble parts to make the whole package reflect what your target market uniquely needs and wants.

CHAPTER

1

What Do You Want to Do With Your Life?

You are so lucky to be a lawyer. Most people get a job—because they need the money—and end up serving that job's purpose for far too many years, or at least until they get their next job.

As a lawyer, while it may not always feel that way, you can write your own ticket. You can create the job you want, wherever you sit. Because career development is mainly just a matter of business development, and vice versa.

- Get hired by a handful of executives to negotiate their employment contracts and you're an employment lawyer.

- Look around and find that your clients are mainly divorced men seeking to retain child custody and you're a fathers' rights lawyer.

- Spend a significant chunk of time negotiating water rights for commercial developments and you're a water rights lawyer.
- Represent young athletes facing disciplinary procedures and ...

Get my drift?

The secret is getting clients who will pay you to do the stuff you are *moved* to do. Maybe you've always harbored a desire to be involved in theater—then figure out how you can do legal work with theater companies, writers, actors and production crews. Perhaps your personal history has created in you a passion for healing broken families—so look at ways you can use your legal capabilities to advocate for the rights of minors in difficult domestic situations.

I once worked with a lawyer who was fond of saying, "Give me 24 hours and the right documents to read, and I can show up in any courtroom in the world and bark like a dog." Meaning, of course, that he thought he was so smart he could fake any kind of expertise. Don't do that. It's important that you cultivate the right kind of real experience, education and skills to practice a specific type of law, not make it up from scratch every time you get a new gig.

But the kind of legal work that you do can, and should, be aligned with your personal mission in life. And that is a great thing—for you and your level of career satisfaction, as well as for the effectiveness and efficiency of your business development activities.

Fill in the Blanks of Your Personal Mission Statement

Chances are, you already know where you want to go—your personal mission. It's that thing you daydream about when you lose interest in what you're actually doing. For the purpose of good business development, you ultimately need to be able to fill in the blanks to complete the following statement:

PERSONAL MISSION STATEMENT:	
So that:	(who)
Can:	(do what)
I will:	(help by)

Let me give you a few examples. (No fair copying someone else's. This is unique to you.)

> So that residents of planned communities in Wisconsin can preserve the unique nature and value of their properties, I will provide legal counsel to homeowners' associations regarding governance, construction, regulation, collection and enforcement.

> So that inventors of new agricultural technologies can retain and benefit from these technologies, I will provide them assistance in acquiring patent and other intellectual property law protection.

> So that high-level professionals from countries outside the United States can take advantage of job opportunities in the Pacific Northwest, I will provide them counsel and advocacy services about work-related visas and naturalization processes.

If you already know the lyrics to this song for yourself, go ahead and fill in the blanks below. If not, resist the temptation to skip ahead to the next section before completing your statement. This step is important: It will show you how to focus your business development activities from here on out. Without focus, you'll have to work a whole lot harder—and even if you're effective and gain new clients, it's a gamble whether it will be satisfying work for you.

Take the time you need to think it through, then complete your own statement. The more narrowly you can define things, the more powerful your business development capability will be—it may seem counterintuitive, but it's true.

PERSONAL MISSION STATEMENT:	
So that:	(who)
Can:	(do what)
I will:	(help by)

This is okay: If you still don't know what you want to do with your life, here's the "cheat" way to fill in the blanks. Identify a very narrow market niche (opportunity) and the services that will be highly saleable within it, and go for that.

This is absolutely NOT okay: It will NOT work for you to say, "I'll do any kind of legal work I can find." Even if you are the rare successful "general practitioner," there must be some way to focus in—age group, geographic area, special language needs. The step is important because it will inform what you do next.

CHAPTER 2

Product Development

Now that you're clear on what you want to do and who you want to do it for, let's see what you know and what you've got to offer them. In essence, you are taking a product to market—and you want to make certain that product is the best it can be, right?

So, taking into consideration what you've identified as your mission, let's ask a few questions:

- Are you, right now, capable and prepared to deliver the services your target market needs and wants? How do you know?

- Can you say you have a really clear understanding of the legal problems to which North Sea fishing fleet owners seek solutions? Hint: If you are basing this on prior representation of a single client or even two, you don't. Not yet.

POINTING IN THE RIGHT DIRECTION **17**

- If you plan to pursue midlife career-changers who are starting their own businesses, do you have a full grasp of the range of business and legal issues you'll confront—and the skills and experience to competently take them on? Sure you've written employment contracts, but what if your client needs to modify a family trust to support the big transition?

- Do you know how public school districts in Arkansas find a lawyer to advise them? Who is generally the district decision-maker—a board, the superintendent? What are the names of the lawyers or firms currently advising districts? Are there regulations that guide the decision to hire lawyers and how they are compensated?

- Where are the bulk of software developers in Idaho physically located and is close physical proximity of their lawyer important to them—or would most be just as happy if all your services were provided virtually?

- Even if you can say you fully understand the dynamics and regulatory environment of legal departments in multinational copper mining companies, can you safely say you know what keeps that general counsel up at night? Hint: Solve that problem and you can pretty much write your own ticket.

Whatever your target market will be, you need to go into information-gathering and learning mode, even if only to discover how much you already know.

- **Use your research skills.** Commit to thoroughly researching the field. It goes without saying that you will need to get (and stay!) up to speed on all legal and regulatory issues of relevance. But for business development purposes, you're also looking for potential clients, competition, public controversies, census information, books, trade associations, blogs ... anything that will help build

> **Even if you can say you fully understand the dynamics and regulatory environment of legal departments in multinational copper mining companies, can you safely say you know what keeps that general counsel up at night?"**

your body of knowledge in the area you have selected. Don't forget to put the contact information of key players you turn up into the contacts spreadsheet you started, including a specific phrase characterizing them (reporter, blogger, association president, Bob Holmes' friend) in the Notes column.

- **Do informational interviews.** Invest a little time in some one-on-one conversations with people representative of your target market. Perhaps they are already clients, or people your current client can introduce you to, or names that turned up in your research. Former clients, spokespeople for the industry, lawyers who work within your target area in other locations, law school professors, or anyone else who may be able to shed light for you on emerging trends, what the market wants and how the legal needs are currently being met. Ask good questions. Listen hard. Make sure you say thank you and reciprocate in some way if you can.

- **Participate.** In many instances, there will be a formal local, national or international association organized around the market you want to serve—the American Institute of Architects-Oregon Chapter, Detroit Regional Chamber of Commerce, American Association for Fathers and Children, American Association of Retired People or the Colorado Mining Association, for example. Sign up and attend a meeting or two. *Listen.* Be a sponge. Ask questions, soak up everything. Take notes. Collect business cards. (Keep adding new people and their information to your contact list.)

Checklist: Getting Ready to Go to Market

By now, you are starting to get a real handle on your specific market, the issues, challenges, trends, secrets, stars—you've asked enough questions to identify both existing legal needs and the possibility that some needs are not being met. Review this checklist and determine what you will need to go to market.

- **Staffing and training.** What do your ideal clients really, really need and what is it going to take for you to provide it for them? If it's expanded capability, should you upgrade or focus your own abilities through learning options like CLE programs, books, internships or college coursework? Or is it going to be a matter of teaming up with, or bringing on board, additional lawyers or other professionals whose capabilities complete the package? Say you're pursuing work with aging high-net-worth individuals: Perhaps building a team that includes medical professionals, tax accountants, business valuation experts and housing specialists will create a whole competitive package of services. A package you'd never be able to provide alone. Or maybe it's simpler and you'll just need a real estate lawyer—or a specialized legal assistant—to complement your own estate planning capabilities.

- **Technology.** Are there ways to improve the efficiency, accuracy, profitability or competitiveness of the services you want to provide by using technology? Perhaps you will offer DIY forms using document automation software or even interactive online services. Through the use of some pretty interesting technologies, you can detour around conventional ways of charging for your services (hourly rates) and benefit competitively by producing solutions for your clients more quickly and cheaply. Don't resist this possibility—explore it! (You can be sure someone else is.)

- **Facilities and location.** What is going to best meet the needs and expectations of your new clients? Think creatively and don't just assume that every lawyer needs the same kind of office with the same kind of desk and the same kind of art on the walls. Where do your clients spend most of their time? Will they come to your office or will you go to theirs? Some lawyers never meet with clients face to face—maybe you will be the one who can get the work done while wearing your pajamas. Maybe your law practice will be in the form of a website. Or be in a strip-mall storefront in the thick of your clients' neighborhood.

- **Packaging.** Consider whether your clients' needs would best be met by packaging several services together. For example, if you plan to pursue work for hospitals, being able to present a hospital-specific legal package that includes the full range of legal services required by a hospital today—provided by a team of lawyers and staff experienced with the range of unique hospital issues and language—would be a requirement. That would include HIPAA and data breaches, physician-hospital relationships, mergers, medical malpractice, tax-exempt compliance, employment and labor concerns, Medicare and more.

- **Pricing.** You need to plan how you will price your services. Figuring out ahead of time whether you will bill by the hour—and your rate—will prevent costly mistakes that can be made when you set fees quickly or too casually. And keep in mind the many pricing models that you can use beyond the billable hour model. Start by asking what will work best for clients. (Ask them!) Then work backward to find a way to make that work for both you and for them.

There will be many, many more things you will need to do to develop your service offering, of course. The next step—understanding fully who is buying your services—will help you refine your to-do list even more.

CHAPTER 3

Who Buys What You Have to Sell?

Remember a few pages back when you explored your personal mission and decided:

"So that _____
can _____
I will _____."

Take that a few steps further now and really home in on your business development targets. Take out a pencil and pad, or pull up OneNote or Evernote, or whatever you use to make notes. Do the following exercise, taking the questions in order. Answer them thoughtfully, drawing on what you learned from your considerable research. In some instances, you will find that you need to do more research.

The Exercise

For the sake of illustration, let's say the work you really want to do can best be described as "business startups" for career changers in mid-level corporate positions. People who are leaving the rat race to launch their own business—new entrepreneurs.

1. **Who hires lawyers to do that kind of work?** Another helpful way to phrase this is: "Who pays money to lawyers to do this work?" Because you want to zoom in on the one person who chooses a lawyer and writes the checks. Following the money is a good way to find out who the real decision-maker is. Right off the bat, this question allows you to carve away a certain percentage of those you might otherwise waste your time on based on your target market. Your potential clients are certainly not in-house counsel with established companies. Nor are they injured individuals looking to sue.

    Generally stated, the people who might hire you to do this type of work are people who are moving in the direction of starting a new business. (I know, duh.) But you can get more specific: inventors, highly specialized professionals who want to bail out of corporate life, B-school grads with a hot idea, younger parents seeking more flexibility for family time. For our purposes, let's choose those people who are tired of what they have to put up with to get a paycheck and want to head out on their own. Give your target a bit more definition, such as age range, geography, language, gender and so on, and you're ready to move on to the next question.

2. **Where do these people get their information?** Assuming Mr. Darcy, Vice President of Human Resources with iZooper Corp. (think of an example of your target market) wants to make an exit in a professional manner, he isn't going to randomly ask around for the names of lawyers who can help him establish his

new business. That might lead to word getting out about his impending departure before he's quite ready. No, he's going to conduct his search for a lawyer in a more sophisticated, confidential fashion. So ask yourself (or ask Google): What do people who want to start their own business read? What blogs are dedicated to their issues? Are there licenses that must be acquired? Does the chamber offer startup packages?

3. **Who has their ear?** You also want to think about types of people who might recommend you to Mr. Darcy. Whose opinion would he value on this question? Now, this is challenging because of concerns about confidentiality, but there will be some people whose recommendation he will value if he can receive it without tipping his own hand about his plans. The list starts with people who have, themselves, left the corporate world and successfully launched a business. How about career counselors who focus on midlife career changers? Their tax advisers?

4. **How can you get in front of those parades?** Here's the payoff for all that research—and where your to-do list begins to develop. Understanding as you now do who might hire you to do simple business startups, you can focus on how to reach them and what to do. In the next section, we'll survey the various methods at your disposal, but here, to prime your thinking, is an example of what that to-do list may include:

    - Join and participate in a couple of LinkedIn groups like On Startups—The Community for Entrepreneurs. Don't lurk. Actively post and participate in online discussions about topics related to the law and business entity creation. Remember, you want to be seen. And you want to be impressive on your topic. If you're not experienced with LinkedIn groups, you'll learn it quickly enough.

> *Once you've focused in on the best activities, you'll be surprised at how simple it is to build a reputation and a network to support getting exactly the kind of work you want. And it's so much easier (and cheaper) than galloping off in all directions!"*

- You've identified a local publication likely read by entrepreneurs (smart people read about where they want to go); now pursue opportunities to write creatively on your topic. (If you live in Colorado, as I do, you'd be looking at the Denver Business Journal.) Find out if there's a chance to develop a series of articles for publication or even a regular column. Be easy to deal with. Write well. Please the editors. They'll want you to write more.

- Volunteer for a local organization focused on training entrepreneurs and new business owners. (Again, in Colorado, you might look at the University of Colorado's Deming Center for Entrepreneurship or Colorado State University's Center for Entrepreneurship.) Talk, teach and write about legal issues related to startup businesses. Do it right, and the people you work with will come to see you as the "business startup lawyer"—and call you when they start up their businesses.

- Write a pamphlet—a downloadable one—and make it available to anyone interested in starting a business. Maybe it's a "how to" or "pitfalls to avoid" guide, or a new business "startup checklist." Promote it via social media and offer it through your website or blog. Tune up your search engine optimization (SEO) so that when Mr. Darcy and others like him Google "starting a business" they'll come upon you.

- Pull together a list of people you have already helped with their businesses and schedule lunches and coffee dates. Find out how their businesses are going now. Build relationships. Network. Introduce these people to others who might help them in their business. And, yes, remind them of your capabilities and ask them to share your name with anyone who may be looking for legal help for their own startup.

There's more—a lot more—you can do, as we will cover in the next segments. Once you've focused in on the best activities, you'll be surprised at how simple it is to build a reputation and a network to support getting exactly the kind of work you want. And it's so much easier (and cheaper) than galloping off in all directions!

PART 2
Exploring the Marketing Menu

By now you should know what you want to do (mission statement), who you want to do it for (target market), and how you will put your services together (product development) to make it attractive to those likely to pay money for your work. With that in mind, it's time to consider the range of possible marketing activities available to you, and then narrow that range to be specific to your plans.

In this segment, you will:

1. Learn about a variety of **marketing tactics** that might help you fulfill your mission.

2. Consider which will be the best and most powerful to **communicate with your unique target market** about your services.

3. Get ready to fill in the blanks to create your **personal marketing plan.**

CHAPTER

4

The Star-Maker Machinery

So here's the idea: You are going to become famous. Not infamous! That would be bad. And not just widely known. That's reality-show territory.

What we're looking for here is earning you a widespread reputation for being really, really good at that one thing you want to do with your life.

Think back to the last time you wanted a doctor with a particular specialty. How did you find her? Perhaps you were referred by your primary care physician. Maybe you read the reviews on Vitals.com or HealthGrades.com. You may have also asked friends or relatives, who gave it some thought and provided the names of the otolaryngologists (or whatever) they knew of.

EXPLORING THE MARKETING MENU 31

And the reason they knew of one is because that one had achieved a level of "fame" in their experience.

That's the kind of fame you want—the kind that means your name is first in mind whenever someone is looking for a lawyer who is really good at that thing you want to do with your life. You want to be *memorable*.

The good news is that the internet makes it a lot easier to become famous than it once was. But, at the same time, it's also way too easy to become famous for something you'd really rather not be known for. So be careful. You may have heard the story about the young professional who tweeted something in unfortunate bad taste as her plane was taking off for Africa, only to learn by the time she arrived that she had been relieved of her job because it went viral. The tools at your disposal make creating a reputation highly doable. But at the same time, missteps can be instantly amplified. So it's important to be thoughtful.

Choose Carefully and Stay Focused!

I was always taught that you can't tell a book by its cover. And life is full of wonderful, surprising examples of just that. Nonetheless, how people look, sound and behave is, rightly or wrongly, how we first assess them and what they do. Take care to project information about yourself that supports your personal mission—that gives the impression that you are indeed what you aspire to be famous for. You want to walk, talk, write, think and work like an expert in your area of focus. And, as you will see in the following pages, there are tons of opportunities for you to do that. Let's prime the pump with these basics.

Speaking. It's hard to beat standing up in front of a group of people who have already self-selected to listen to you on a topic in which they are interested as a chance to impress on the right people your experience and competence. By the stories you tell, the knowledge you impart, the names you drop and your general appearance of confidence and familiarity with your subject, you will convey what you are known for with the authority of the podium.

Writing. You may think writing for publication is like public speaking, only sitting down and without the stage fright. But it can be so much more. Whether writing for print or digital, association publications or conference proceedings, a handbook or pamphlet, tweet or blog—your writing can be leveraged, rewritten, reformatted, sliced, diced, polished, perfected and shared to communicate exactly what you want. And what your readers want. You do it through strategic content management—the digital *content* involved may be images, video, audio and multimedia as well as text.

Joining. You are known by the company you keep. When someone is a member of the American Medical Association, it's assumed she is a doctor. If you are a member of the Public Contract Law Section of the American Bar Association, you may counsel defense contractors and defense agencies or recipients of federal and state grants. Join the Silicon Valley Intellectual Property Law Association or feature the Association of Zoos and Aquariums in your bio and the relevant assumptions will be made.

Giving. Most lawyers make charitable contributions within their community. If you are donating time, skill or money to an entity related to your area of legal practice, you will not only meet people with whom you can share information and introductions, you will also be perceived as someone who is interested in and working within that substantive area. Obviously you don't want to be cynical about this and only give time or money out of a desire to get clients. But chances are that, if the kind of work you seek really moves you, you'll find charitable opportunities that meet both needs simultaneously.

Collaborating. You don't always have to be the star of your own movie to gain recognition. Co-writing an article or sharing the podium with an expert in a particular field (a client, perhaps?) can reinforce the impression that you play in the stars' ballgame. That you are an expert, too, by association.

Promoting. And, of course, there are all kinds of direct ways to communicate your expertise—brochures, websites, blogs, fact sheets, Q&A sites, directories, news releases and more.

Now, as we explore a range of marketing tactics, view them through the lens of your target market and try to choose the most direct, effective methods that will push you toward your goal. By constantly checking options against your personal mission and the target market you wish to serve, some decisions will already be made for you.

CHAPTER
5

You, Online

You know what type of lawyer you want the world to see in you, so find the baseline. Who does the world see right now when it looks at you through the online lens? What's your online persona? A huge part of creating the practice you want begins with cultivating your online "avatar"—this is where you plant the seeds and grow your reputation.

So let's get started. Pull up the search box at Google.com. Type in your name in quotation marks and hit enter. (Run the search twice if you use different versions of your name—say, with a middle or maiden name.) And there you are. That's how you look to a stranger seeking information about you. What kind of impression do you make?

You'll find the good stuff over which you've had some control: your LinkedIn profile, your firm's website, complete with lovely photo and bio, links to articles you've published, blog posts you've written, speeches you're scheduled to make. You'll find the big lawyer directories. (Wonder what they have to say about you?) You'll also find some surprises, such as unsolicited online reviews of your services by former and existing clients. Maybe even a few from former employees. (Hope they're good!)

But there will also be some things you wish weren't there: Facebook photos tagged by others. Inappropriate Instagram selfies you actually posted yourself. (Why?!) Ancient news items, links that go nowhere or, worse, that connect to dicey sites. Letters to the editor. Complaints to city council.

Is there no end? It can seem that way. Merely one version of my own name right now brings up 1,750 hits! No client in his right mind will go through all of them. But all it takes is a couple of bad ones.

Ask Some Questions

If I do that search on your name and rummage through a few pages of hits, the nature of your practice should become obvious. Will it?

Can I tell from the list of articles, speeches, biographies and news items that you are a Virginia litigator focused on Big Tobacco and mesothelioma defense—just as you want? Or will you look more like a lawyer who has bounced all over the place in the past two decades—trademarks, Brownfields, oil and gas, and the five years you spent as special master on construction disputes? There's nothing wrong with any of that, but if you're presenting yourself as a Big Tobacco defense guy, be prepared to respond to questions about why you've been so fickle and how those skills translate. (And think hard next time before accepting that invitation to speak at a conference about trends in uncontested divorce law.)

Or maybe when I run that search, you will look like someone who doesn't care what the world thinks about her. Three different LinkedIn profiles with your name on them, but none with a photo, and none with complete information? Five years since you've posted on that blog you started? Have you neglected to provide current contact information to online directories or professional associations, resulting in five different email addresses with three different firms?

Or perhaps I will stumble onto the side of you that you'd rather keep from clients' eyes. No client wants to know you celebrate July 14 by dressing as Marie Antoinette and storming the local brewpub. Or that your Star Wars name is Bulsar Vulan. While you don't want to completely sanitize your personality, certain things just don't shout "effective professional," or leave the impression you'll understand the importance of a client's concern.

Checklist: Clean Up Your Act

The good news is that now you have a focus. So, before you jump into doubling your Twitter followers, branching into Tumblr or launching a YouTube channel, get your current act cleaned up. Do a sweep of every social network where you have an account.

- **Get squeaky clean.** Go back in time and eliminate rough language or references. You know what I'm talking about. Not just on Facebook and Twitter, either. Photo-sharing sites such as Flickr, Instagram, Tumblr and Pinterest, as well as video-sharing sites such as YouTube, may contain unflattering content. While you are checking, watch for language that may run afoul of ethics rules.

- **Hush it up.** Learn about privacy settings and change them to support the brand, or personal image, you seek to project. Don't get too heavy-handed, though—people like to know you're hip to the internet and not a trembling wad of social media paranoia.

- **Update everything.** Make certain your bios and profiles are totally up to date. Schedule time to update them regularly. Publish something new? Elected to head a nonprofit board? Changed your name? It all needs to be current. And consistent.

- **Put a good face on it.** Replace your headshot on the social networking sites with something a little more current—and not something taken with a smartphone. Look as professional as you are. Pay for a good photo that conveys exactly what you want to project.

- **Redecorate.** Most social media sites provide a way to personalize your page with cover and background images. Do it. But be tasteful—the image tells people something about you. (Probably not an Oakland Raiders skull and crossbones fan shot—unless they are your client.) Keep it fresh. Here's an incentive: Every time you change your cover image on Facebook, the new one rolls by in your friends' newsfeed, providing another opportunity for you to reconnect with people. Or not.

- **Who loves ya?** You are who you hang out with. Maybe it's time to do a little housecleaning among your followers and friends?

- **Visit competitors' profiles.** What does she look like? How much information does he share? Take a tour (do it periodically). Potential clients will compare you, so why not know what you're up against?

CHAPTER

6

Your Website

You must have a website for your law practice. Period. It is the hub around which all other marketing materials and activities revolve. And you're just plain not credible if you can't be found on the internet.

If you practice in a firm of any size, the firm's website is likely not your responsibility. But you are responsible for maximizing the effectiveness of the pages that describe you and your practice. Track down the primary author of your firm's site for assistance, to ensure your practice pages are complete, up to date and (to the extent possible) aligned with your personal mission statement.

Lawyers who practice on their own, though, will have responsibility for creating and maintaining a website that gives their practice a dynamic presence on the web. There are any number of ways you may go about this: Hire a consultant or contractor, do it yourself, involve a skilled family member, or sign on with a custom lawyer website service like Lawyers.com, JurisPage or Websites for Lawyers. But ideally, it will be impossible to tell the size of your firm by looking at your materials. Being a small entity doesn't give you a free pass on looking unsophisticated and cheap.

At an absolute minimum, your website must include:

- A personal biography
- A truly great photo of yourself (don't skimp here!)
- A description of services that you offer (in plain English)
- Contact information
- Links to your social media accounts (Twitter, Facebook, LinkedIn)
- A means for sharing articles, news items and posts

Other things that are nice to have include:

- A blog
- Contact tracking and intake form

Start with your personal mission and target market in mind and craft your site to suit. So many subliminal messages can be sent unintentionally. If your target market is general counsel with international corporations, they won't stay on your site long if the grunge graphics, colors and text conspire to better appeal to a millennial T-shirt vendor. Worse, if your site appears cheap and amateurish, with too many fonts and selfies instead of professional photography, you will give the impression that you are amateurish about the practice of law as well.

Choosing a URL for your website is one of the most important marketing decisions you will make. It must be short, unique, simple, easy to remember, and representative of who you are or what you do. If you are combining several words, make certain they don't spell something else entirely when joined together. (Warning: Make sure that you own the domain, not your website host or marketing firm.) Include your URL everywhere you place your contact information.

If at all possible, make sure your site is optimized for mobile, that it scales well from device to device upon which a person will view it. And update your site with fresh information constantly.

CHAPTER

7

Content Marketing

I've got good news and ... er, weird news. First the weird: Whether you like it or not, you have become a media outlet.

If you don't believe me, think for a minute about all the stuff—pictures, posts, emails, videos, opinions, reviews—that you shoot out through the internet each day. Even if all you do is Facebook vacation photos, you are a source of "content" for your public just like HBO, The New York Times and The Daily Beast.

And as with those media outlets, your audience will draw conclusions about you based on what they read, hear and view—via you. In the same way people know The Onion is a source of wacky (okay, occasionally offensive) humor and Fox News tends to have a politically conservative take on the world, the people who are privy to your content know things and have opinions about you, too.

EXPLORING THE MARKETING MENU **43**

The good news? This is not a bad thing. Because you can manage all of the various content you share in a way that tells the world what you want it to know about you. That's called "content marketing."

The Content Marketing Institute defines it as "a marketing technique of creating and distributing valuable, relevant and consistent content to attract and acquire a clearly defined audience—with the objective of driving profitable customer action."

There are literally hundreds of different ways to push your content out into the world. Some are brought to you by the wonders of the internet. Others require your in-person participation. Some are free for the taking and require nothing beyond the creation of dynamite content. Others, such as advertising and some directory listings, will cost money, but can be very worth the expense if well-targeted to the proper consumers.

Social Media

If you aren't already active in several forms of social media—well, that's very surprising. These communication platforms have become astoundingly influential, not just as places to chat, but also to form communities, connect, teach and learn, and identify trends. So let's assume you're fairly conversant and identify the social media sites where you must be present: Facebook, Twitter and LinkedIn. Mindful that social media is reinventing itself constantly, with the various platforms competing to offer new and better features and functions daily, here's where most lawyers are now:

- LinkedIn is the professional directory where anyone half worth their resume can be found. Your level of participation can range from passive (a simple profile page) to very active—via a subject area group, regular Pulse articles, frequent updates and sharing of information, personal referrals from clients and colleagues, and ample usage of add-ins like SlideShare to reuse content from other media. Your return on investment from LinkedIn will correlate directly to your level and quality of effort.

- Twitter has become something akin to a public shared consciousness, constantly updated with items trivial, profound, newsworthy and preposterous. It can be used by a professional like yourself to build a public profile for your interests and areas of expertise by regularly tweeting links to your own material (as well as others'). As with all social media, there are specific rules of behavior and style that should be observed. You will be sorely judged if you blare advertising-like tweets, but rewarded with growing respect if your tweets can be counted on for good substance and appropriate etiquette. Primarily, focus on building your number of followers in your target market, following others who are part of the community you seek to identify with, and providing quality tweets and retweets on pertinent topics.

- Facebook, of the big three, is the most casual platform. Casual can be fine, but be mindful that strict privacy settings are necessary to limit your visibility if you don't want potential clients or referrers to see those Halloween beer pong pictures from college. To avoid that possibility, some professionals choose to reserve their Facebook presence for family news and interaction with friends. Ideally, you will feel comfortable enough to build honest friendships with other professionals online because, as we are so often reminded, effective business development is built on a base of good relationships.

Other platforms, including Pinterest, Instagram, Google+, Tumblr and more, can be appropriate places to share content, depending on your area of focus. Very few in-house counsel get their information from Pinterest at this juncture, for example. But it is important to track social media trends for new developments and evolving opportunities. So go ahead, hit the web and see which of today's options matches with your target audience.

Writing for Periodicals and Blogs

Writing for publication is a time-honored tradition in the legal profession. Lawyers are good with words—although writing for a law review is not the same as writing for popular consumption. One of the traits you will be valued for by clients and referral sources is your ability to simplify and translate legal language. Writing an article or blog posts is your opportunity to demonstrate that.

Area-specific print magazines and journals, industry or association blogs and online publications all offer great opportunities to target where your content is going. For example, Physicians Practice magazine is read by doctors who are concerned about managing the business of their medical practice. An employment lawyer's article about staff termination practices would be well placed there. Equally well received would be articles about HIPAA requirements and texting, agreements with insurance payers, or possible recourse when a patient defames a doctor online. If the article about staff terminations contains information that's applicable in other, non-medical workplaces, it could be revised slightly and reused for publication in practice management periodicals for engineers, architects, accountants and even lawyers.

You might also produce your own blog, newsletter or client bulletin. Or, you could participate in a multi-author blog. When you write a blog post or publish an article online, you can share the link via Facebook, Twitter and LinkedIn accounts—and other people can share the link, too. Publish something in an online magazine and then push it out to people by tweeting and posting about it on Facebook and LinkedIn.

Having your own blog covering a niche where no other publication lives is a particularly fine form of content marketing. Tom Goldstein's SCOTUSblog.com (United States Supreme Court), Bill Marler's

MarlerBlog.com (food-borne illnesses litigation) and Julie Fershtman's EquineLawBlog.com (horse industry) are great examples.

Direct Mail and Email Marketing

In the past, lawyers would photocopy articles they had written, then slip them into envelopes to mail to people on their contact list. Some still do it this way, and there is something to be said for a personal handwritten note attached to a nicely reproduced article. But, for the most part, this kind of mailing now takes the form of email.

Most publishers will provide you with a PDF that reproduces the layout and design of the original piece. You can attach the PDF of your article to a personal email message or take advantage of email marketing services like Constant Contact or MailChimp. These services will manage your lists and deliver beautifully designed email messages or complete email newsletters, sharing the content in full or leading the reader to click through to your material. Email marketing services can also be used to collect information from your website's contact forms, generating custom, automated messages to anyone who submits their information through your website.

Self-Publishing Projects

Many lawyers produce brochures or how-to booklets about the particular areas of law in which they practice. A tip sheet or how-to guide can be very powerful. For example, it's easy to imagine some of these helpful publications for clients: "So You've Decided to Buy Your First House" (for a general small town practice), "What You Need to Know About Child Custody in Minnesota" (family practice), "The Affordable Care Act: A Guide to Compliance Issues" (labor and employment law) or "Keep Your Trademark Safe: 10 Tips for Proper Use" (intellectual property law).

Another way to distribute content that affirms your competence in a particular area while also providing a service to current and potential clients is to produce periodic client newsletters or alerts. If your practice area is subject to frequent changes in case law, it may be a simple matter to draft quick plain-English descriptions of new developments that may change the ways business is conducted and send them via email to people who have opted in to receive them.

You can even write the book! There's a reason that "He wrote the book" is a euphemism for knowing everything there is to know about a topic. Anyone capable of spending the time and energy to write a whole book on a topic must (1) know an awful lot and (2) have a significant dedication to their field.

Finding a willing publisher for your expert tome can be a challenge. On the other hand, you can easily self-publish via online services. There's a lot to book publishing, so lay your hands on some helpful resources like Guy Kawasaki and Shawn Welch's book, "APE (Author, Publisher, Entrepreneur)—How to Publish a Book."

Podcasts, Webcasts and Video

Of course, it's not always a matter of putting pen to paper or fingers to keyboard. By participating in podcasts, webcasts and video productions—or producing your own—you can show off the same smarts that written content would showcase, *and* it's a good way to demonstrate your personal affability, intellect and communication skills. A family lawyer might, for example, produce a video coaching fathers on what to expect in child custody cases.

You might offer a special how-to webcast to existing clients, post an educational video on YouTube or include streaming video as part of your website or blog, for example.

Content Syndicators

Content syndication services are widely used by large law firms, and there's no reason why individual lawyers can't benefit from this means of distributing content beyond their own circle of known contacts. Syndication services, for a price, will distribute your material directly to the inboxes of a wide range of readers who have specifically indicated their interest in the subject or industry area that you address. Readers' access is nearly always free of charge. You won't have to worry about managing your list or direct-mail bloopers with this kind of service. Some of the most popular syndicators among lawyers are currently JDSupra, Mondaq, Lexology and The National Law Review.

Leveraging Content

This is only a sampling of ways you can display what you know and share content that demonstrates your areas of knowledge. There are others and you will discover or create ways that are a perfect fit for your focus. One important thing to remember is that you should be using a variety of media at all times and that you must use each to leverage off the others. Tweet about what you post in your blog. Blog about the book you've just published. Let people know via email alerts and LinkedIn postings when you will be speaking at an important conference. The sum of the whole will always be greater than the collection of the parts—if managed properly!

CHAPTER 8

Tips for Making More Impact With Your Content

You may feel confident that you are an excellent writer. Heck, you're a law school graduate, right? Well, creating content for your target market is a different animal—and it will help to review a few tips to keep your writing fresh and powerful.

Don't write like a lawyer. Check your whereases, heretofores and notwithstandings at the door. Avoid jargon. Often, a new lawyer will feel he must impress and intimidate. It's a common newbie mistake.

The truth is that the best lawyers—and certainly the best client-getters—comfortably write and speak in plain English, opting for understanding over intimidation. Sure, you must know and understand all the complexities of the law, that's assumed by virtue of the J.D. after your name. But every client wants a lawyer who can communicate clearly with her.

Write to your audience. Having pinpointed the focus of your practice, it should be an easy matter now to identify the precise demographic you want to draw to your content. Municipal water law? City managers. Trade secrets and covenants not to compete? In-house counsel and human resources executives of emerging technology companies. A piece on food regulations in the Mississippi Grocer will do you more good than an article in the Mississippi Bar Journal. Having identified them, develop and provide content that is important, useful and powerful to just those people. Oh, yes, take into consideration style as well as subject matter. You'll write very differently for couples considering collaborative divorce than you will for CEOs of multinational corporations.

Only create content about things worth talking about. A person can go crazy saying yes to every invitation to write or speak. So don't. The secret to controlling both your time and your message is to put content out there that relates to the specific subject matter you want to focus your practice on. So you want to focus on regulatory takings? Politely decline invitations to speak to your church group about revocable trusts (though yes, we know you'd do a bang-up job). Instead, hand off the invitation to a lawyer you know who specializes in trusts and estates. She'll owe you one. And you'll stay focused.

Create once, use many times. If you do the hard work to give a speech and then just drag your notes into a folder when it's over, you've missed the boat. Leverage the time you spent developing expertise in the topic by repurposing the information you collected for the speech:

- Draft a feature article for submission to an industry publication.
- Tweet a link to the article when it publishes, and don't forget to add it to your LinkedIn profile.
- Write and publish a short post for your blog on a related topic—again, don't forget to Tweet the link to your published article and add it to your LinkedIn profile.
- Post a video on your website giving the speech—and use social media to link to the video post.
- Use the initial speech along with input from people in the audience to create an outline for an e-book. Self-publish or submit it to an industry association or trade publisher for consideration.
- Include the speech, article, post and video in your bio on your firm's website. With links.

Set the hook. It's an old journalism term. When writing a story, it's important to "set the hook" in your first few sentences—hooking readers in so they will want to know more. It requires you to get into your readers' heads, figure out what's really itching, then write about the thing that will scratch that itch for them. If you're building content, don't waste your time on fluff. Instead, deliver material that is topical and close to emerging issues. Content marketing experts are fond of saying that every morsel of content is like dropping a hook in the sea for new clients. Make sure you bait it with something delectable.

Change it up. Start with the assumption that everything (Every. Thing.) you do in online marketing must be interactive. Meaning don't limit your content to text. A good mix of different kinds of content—images, infographics, audio, video and text—draws your audience in. They'll also be more likely to share with others. And don't forget you have to constantly feed the voracious appetite of your followers with new content. Because they always want more, but also because a flow of good helpful material keeps their minds on you and undistracted by others.

Speak your market's language. Every industry has its own unique idioms, turns of phrase, familiar buzzwords, inside references. If you are writing to connect with a specific group, be one of them. You are more likely to be hired by someone if you speak the language she connects with.

Simplify. Write to create understanding, not to show how much you know. Your reader will not care how much you know, as long as you demonstrate that you know that one thing in which she is interested. Shorter words are better. Starting a sentence with "however" is just a silly way to avoid starting with "but." "In the event that ..." is just dumb. Say "if." "In order to" is two too many words. Just say "to." Avoid passive voice. Period.

Find someone *without* legal experience to review and comment. Seriously. You're not asking for feedback on your technical legal knowledge, you just want to know how understandable it is to someone who doesn't know about all that stuff. This isn't about being a good lawyer. It's about being a communicator.

Proofread. If there are stains on the tray table, an airline passenger will assume poor engine maintenance. The same goes for a lawyer's writing. Most clients don't know good lawyering from bad. They only know results. And while they don't know good legal writing, they do know typos and grammatical errors. You can bet they will make assumptions accordingly. Lingofy.com and Grammarly.com will proofread the content you create in web browsers, helping to find errors in spelling, usage and style as you post to WordPress, Blogger, Twitter, Tumblr, Facebook and more.

Read. People who read a lot tend to write well. Make it a habit to read lots of different styles of writing—promotional, fiction, technical, essays, storytelling—so you'll grow more adept at writing in different styles for different purposes.

CHAPTER
9

Marketing Materials

In addition to your own wonderful self, your firm's website and any social media avatars that speak in your voice online, you're going to need some communication tools to tell the world about you and your capabilities. Why? Because:

- There are some things better communicated this way than you flapping your lips. A list of clients, say, or your contact information.

- It gets the basics out of the way and leaves your in-person time for really personalized interaction.

- A well-produced batch of materials subliminally reinforces your level of professionalism and sets the tone for your practice.

- You can tailor information that will be provided to potential clients in advance to create exactly the image you want. Having seen your materials, by the time you are actually reaching out to shake a hand, they should already be impressed with you.

- Making information available 24 hours a day (online or on their desk) means potential clients have access to information about you.

If you practice in a firm of any size, there will already be templates and best practices in place to help you with this. Just find the person in the firm who is responsible for marketing activities and ask what they need to help you put things together. If you're practicing on your own, or even in a small firm, preparing these items will fall to you.

The Basics: In Their Hands

Let's start with the things you absolutely need for clients and potential clients.

Business card. You must have something to hand over when you meet a potential client, referral source, colleague, new acquaintance or vendor. Make sure it says the right thing about you. Quality paper equals a quality lawyer, for example. A business card's job is to put your contact info in their hands—including your website URL. Make sure it does the job clearly. Some lawyers handwrite their personal cell number on the card right before handing it over. It's a gesture that communicates you think this person is really important. Some lawyers put their picture on their business cards, the thinking being that if someone collects cards from several people at an event, having your picture will help them remember you.

Biography. This is where you tell people who you are and why they should refer or engage you. Remember in this book's first section you gathered together every item of information about your education and experience? That's the place to start when you draft your bio. Where you went to school, papers you've published, speeches you've given and awards you've won are relevant. But the most important thing is a description of the type of services you provide—from the perspective of the client. Note: If you want to include client names in relation to cases you've been involved in, make sure you ask those clients for permission.

You'll want your polished biography handily available in paper and digital format. And for most lawyers, there should be several different versions tailored to different targets. I'm not suggesting you disguise yourself as something you aren't, just that different kinds of experience and capabilities should be emphasized based on how the information will be used and who it is intended for. If you're a solo whose general practice is broad, for example, you'll need a biography for criminal law and a separate one for family law.

Useful Electives

There is so much more you can do to provide contacts, potential clients and clients with the information they need about you and your practice. Here are just a few things to consider, depending on how well they lend themselves to your practice focus and market. Of course, any or all of these can be produced in a print or digital format.

Case studies. You will need permission from any players in a case history in order to use actual names of people and organizations. If you can't get permission, or you'd rather not, "anonymize" the description by changing the name of a company to something like "Large national paper box manufacturer" and identify individual players with the name of their role, such as CEO or plaintiff.

Articles you have written. Whenever you get an article published, ask the magazine, paper, blog, whatever, for a formal reprint. This should include the masthead of the publication at the top of the page above your article (with none of their other articles) in PDF form so you can print it out or attach it to an email. If they can't make that available, mock one up yourself by cutting and pasting.

Client feedback. Over time, you will receive compliments and positive feedback from clients and others. If it's in writing, save it! Delivered orally? Write it down. Hearing nothing but knowing they are happy, ask if they would be willing to write a letter (or email) with feedback. Drop all of this great material into a single document as you receive it. You may use this information as a simple "What Others Say About Me" document, feature some quotes on your website, or include particularly relevant remarks in proposals or cover letters.

Resource lists. It's possible that there are some really good resources available to people with problems in your area of practice. Help them out and develop a list to share. Put your name on the list, of course, and they will remember how helpful you are. One environmental lawyer created a single sheet translator of all the critical regulatory acronyms (CERCLA, RCRA, NEPA, etc.) and it "went viral." A great way to create name recognition among the exact crowd you want to know about you!

Slide shows. When you do a speaking engagement (more on these later) and prepare written materials or a slide deck on a particular topic, don't forget to make nice copies to be included in information packets, or preserve them in a specific file with other speech materials so you can draw on them later. You can also post them on your website, LinkedIn or SlideShare.

CHAPTER
10

Joining the Right Organization

One of the best ways—if not *the* best way—to find potential clients and referral sources that match your target market criteria is to join and participate in trade, professional and social organizations with a focus.

If, for example, you are an environmental lawyer seeking to help Alaskan gold-mine owners develop their placer mining holdings within the law, what better place to invest time and effort than the Alaskan Mining Association? By participating in statewide and branch events you'll meet members who include mining executives, prospectors, developers, geoscientists and consultants. Perfect! They've already self-selected for you.

Or suppose you are an employment lawyer interested in developing and providing training programs on the legal issues related to diversity in international companies. It would make perfect sense for you to pursue involvement with the Society for Human Resource Management (SHRM), the world's largest membership organization devoted to human resource management. It has more than 275,000 members in over 160 countries around the world.

The more focused the organization's purpose is—and the more closely aligned with your target market it is—the more successful you are likely to be at developing new business because of your involvement. Often, lawyers join the local chamber of commerce or Rotary Club, but find it's unproductive because the focus of the group's membership is so broad. That doesn't mean the chamber and Rotary aren't good organizations to support, only that your expectations for them need to be modest if you offer a very specialized legal service to a very narrow market. If your practice focuses on partnership agreements in medical practices, try organizations focused on doctors. But if your ideal client is a small local business, the chamber might be right for you.

Joining Isn't Enough

If the association or club you join has more than 10 members, you aren't going to find the visibility you deserve by merely paying membership dues, and your investment won't pay off as it should. Once you sign on, attend a meeting or two, read the regular publications and follow any electronic or snail-mail conversations. Basically, you are casing the joint. You'll want to figure out what makes the group run, where the power lies and where the action happens. Then, get more involved.

Introduce yourself to the president or executive director and let them know you are interested in investing some of your time to benefit the goals of the organization. Join a sub-group or committee. Ask who they think you should meet. Volunteer to speak at a luncheon—but don't overdo it. Every organization executive is aware of those self-serving members who sign up only to see what the organization can do for them. (Behind closed doors, those members are often the subject of derision, rarely thought of for juicy opportunities.) You need to demonstrate your commitment to benefiting the organization and helping its members.

There are many ways to be visibly involved in your new organization:

Committees. This is where you show off your ability to get things done and make good things happen. This is what people will look for when they need a lawyer, regardless of your area of specialty. A program committee can offer opportunities to contact high-profile people and build your contact list. Fundraising committees really keep you close to the most important—and visible to leadership—work of any organization. The newsletter or publications committee can give you the chance to keep your name in the public eye, especially if you are a skillful writer.

Pro bono legal work. Maybe this group needs help with new bylaws language or wants to protect its intellectual property. Business societies confront any number of legal issues that may lend themselves to your considerable capabilities. Or the board of directors may want someone to sit in with them for meetings about issues touching on law. Wouldn't it be great if they could all say "She sure did a great job for us!" when someone asked?

Special projects. Could you liaise for the group with another similar organization you know? Help with a member survey? Develop guidelines for some new activity?

> ❝ *If you are complimented on something you have done and know that someone else helped, make sure that person publicly receives the praise as well. Share the credit!"*

Other kinds of contributions. Can you offer your firm's conference room as a meeting space? Maybe you can bring a high-profile speaker (you just happen to know from elsewhere) to the group, or offer your staff's administrative services to support a special project or an election. If you keep your eyes open for opportunities, you'll find them.

Officer positions or board memberships. Obviously you won't be able to jump right in and become president—and that job might be more of an investment of time than you have in mind!—but if you participate in committees, write for publications, demonstrate your ability to make things happen and have a generally positive profile and relationships within the organization, it won't be long before you are asked to take a leadership role. Then you will be widely known and appreciated in the way that lawyers who receive great referrals are.

Mind Your Manners

The goal of joining an organization is to meet a lot of people who have the potential to hire or refer you. You want to build positive relationships, make introductions, share information and generally help other members to succeed. To that end, here are just a few rules of the road for the uninitiated.

Honor the organization's decision-making system. Don't go over someone's head to get action without first involving them. Otherwise, you will have made yourself at least one enemy.

Pay your dues—in both senses. Yes, you should always pay your membership fees on time, if not before. And if there's an opportunity to make a charitable contribution and you can, do it. But also remember that, as with any new community, you must "pay your dues" before you get to the really good stuff. So, just like when you start a new job, be willing to roll up your sleeves and do the work no one else will do. With a smile. Those you have helped will be invested in your success if they see you as a "good guy."

Keep confidences. Just say no to gossip. And if you are invited into closed meetings, keep the information from the meeting to yourself.

Be humble. If you are complimented on something you have done and know that someone else helped, make sure that person publicly receives the praise as well. Share the credit!

Be respectful of association staff. Many smaller organizations don't have any staff whatsoever, and the administrative work is handled by members. But those of any size will have an executive director and more. If you are rude to the staff meeting planner—take credit for what he did, ignore instructions, go over her head—that black mark against your name will come back to haunt you. If you are helpful to staff—contribute proofreading services, help develop a database, answer tough questions when no one else will—they will work behind the scenes to help you find opportunities. Never underestimate the clout a staff member holds.

Speak well of the group. It's your gang. Be proud of it. Advocate for it. Be willing to serve as a reference for it. Use your reputation to gain speakers and exhibitors. Caveat: If you can't speak well of it, don't speak of it at all to outsiders. Work from the inside to make it something you and others can be proud of.

CONVENE YOUR OWN CLUB

Maybe you've looked but can't find a professional, trade or community organization that is a good match for the focus of your practice. Don't fret. This may be one of the best opportunities yet. Unless your practice is dedicated to some incredibly arcane bit of legal minutiae from the Dark Ages of Swedish alchemy, you are probably not the only one looking to gather with others who are interested in this area. And by serving as the catalyst to create the gathering opportunity, you can literally own it. A few examples:

Scotch and potato chips. Fred was a very senior litigator in a big law firm. Most of his clients were multinational mining and oil companies with significant physical interests in his region of the country—the Rocky Mountains. Over the years, he and his colleagues had handled many cases involving an important issue peculiar to the western U.S.: ownership of water rights. Along the way, he grew to believe that some of his clients' problems could be eliminated if their companies could collaborate on development of new law. He asked representatives of each of the highest profile companies to join him one Friday afternoon for Scotch and potato chips (he had always found wine and cheese sort of snobby) to discuss it. The discussion went so well—resulting in changes in regulation that did indeed simplify water rights issues and result in major cost savings for all involved—that the group decided to continue meeting once a quarter to enjoy Scotch and potato chips with collegial and professional conversation.

Cross-professional discussion and training. Many areas of law involve technical experts and professionals from fields outside the law. If there is a way for this diverse group to organize themselves as equals for professional and social exchanges, it can provide professional development, networking opportunities and lots of other good things. Rosemary realized that there was a small informal local community of lawyers, engineers, scientists and regulators who always showed up at public hearings, PRP meetings, seminars and anything else related to her hazardous materials practice. The names on request for proposal routing lists and expert witness directories were nearly always familiar ones. So when new CERCLA law was finalized and the EPA offered training webinars, she volunteered her firm's conference room for a group viewing and discussion. It went so well that she started scheduling and publicizing other training presentations over the lunch hour and attendance grew. Eventually, an organization was formalized—bylaws, officers and everything—into a statewide association that met monthly, distributed a newsletter, and hosted a two-day annual conference and trade show.

Out of sight, but not out of mind. If there isn't anything close to a critical mass in your locale given your narrow field of focus, consider what Perry did. He is a solo trademark lawyer in a midsize city. Most of his clients are marketing professionals, publishers and advertising agencies. One challenge of solo practice is the limited nature of your resources, particularly when it comes to clients who need assistance in other states or other countries. Perry created a network of solo trademark lawyers throughout North America to help him respond to client needs or referrals. He and a couple of other key players took responsibility for organizing regular exchanges of information and CLE programs among the participants. Ultimately they were holding biannual meetings in various locations specifically designed to educate their clients as well as themselves—and to enjoy some connection-building social time together. In addition to the expected referrals, Perry's leadership role in the organization gave him high visibility nationally, built his profile in the eyes of his clients, and potential clients and added an impressive credential to his CV.

Every specialized group has to start somewhere. You might as well be the one who gets the ball rolling.

CHAPTER 11

Finding the Right Speaking Engagements

Public speaking is one of the best anchors for business development activities. Not only does it allow you to show off your knowledge and experience, but people in your audience can assess your personal style, likeability and communication style as well.

Which isn't to say that public speaking isn't hard work. It certainly can be—particularly for those who dread standing up before groups of strangers. And those who insist on doing a really good job. (That should be you, by the way.) So don't waste your time and energy by speaking to just any old group. Make sure you are speaking to the right group—your target market. That means people who either hire lawyers like you to do work you

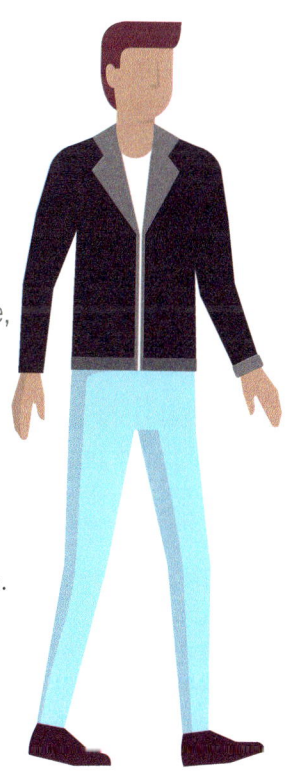

EXPLORING THE MARKETING MENU **69**

have identified as your goal, or people who refer potential clients for that kind of work.

So what kind of speaking engagements do you want? Here are five criteria to use.

- **Exposure to the right type of people.** You want to make certain the people in the room are interested in what you have to say because they could hire or refer people like you. This doesn't mean you shouldn't speak at your child's Career Day program. Just don't count it as business development—those 10-year-olds aren't prospective clients.

- **Settings that show you off to advantage.** If you're just starting out, you may not have a lot of public speaking experience. But in a very short while, you will learn which situations are most comfortable for you and when you get the best feedback. Panel discussion? Roundtable conversation? Keynote speech? Group facilitation? Small group? Large? Once you begin to figure it out, focus in on and ask for speaking opportunities structured to take advantage of your strengths.

- **Opportunities that could lead to more opportunities to speak.** Often, if you do a good job, you will be approached by someone from the audience who thinks you should give this same speech to a different group. Bingo!

- **Descriptions that will look good on your CV.** There will be some speaking opportunities that don't actually get you in front of buyers of your special type of legal services but do provide a good credential. Being asked to present on your area of specialty to a law school class at Harvard would look pretty good even if there's little chance those students would refer work to you. You will have to judge the tradeoff.

- **Doing a favor for a client or potential client.** Say you've been wooing the vice president of human resources at a company for months—you're interested in taking over their age-discrimination cases. Out of the blue, he asks if you'd be willing to speak to the board of directors of a community organization he chairs. The answer is, "You bet I would!" Even if the directors are far from being potential clients, it's a chance to do something nice for the VP and continue to build a relationship.

How Do Lawyers Get These Gigs?

It's true, some lawyers are so popular as speakers, they have to practically beat off requests with a stick. Hone your presentation skills and keep at it, and your time will come. Meanwhile it's your job to build a reputation that will attract invitations. Here are some steps to take.

- **Figure out where your target market convenes.** Professional and trade associations are perfect speaking venues. Follow them and track events as they are planned.

- **Be a participant first.** Volunteer your time and resources to help with conferences, luncheons and anything else that relates to your target market. Demonstrate your reliability and professionalism. Do the hard work and people will want to help you get ahead. Don't presume you are automatically entitled to an invitation to speak. No matter how smart or famous you are, your opportunities will always grow in relation to your willingness to contribute at any level.

- **Ask.** Make it your business to know how speakers are selected and who does the selecting. Mark your calendar for upcoming deadlines for speaking proposals. Make sure the selection people know about you and have information about your topic and your capabilities.

- **Write about your topic.** Being a published expert doesn't hurt. Think back to the writing and content tips from earlier sections of this book. If you don't have a blog, consider starting one. It is a good way to position yourself as an expert—you are in charge and can write about the trends in your area and the hot topics that conference planners search for.

- **Do a truly great job every time you speak.** You never know when your capabilities are being judged. If you can build a reputation for excellent preparation, interesting (and entertaining) presentation and delivery of cutting-edge information, it will be noticed. Make the conference planner's job a pleasure.

- **Be a thought leader.** Choose your topics wisely. Keep them focused, topical and up to date. Hot topics get a lot of attention, and if you can be visible speaking on them before others are, you'll be a shoo-in for that next speaking invitation.

- **Be there!** Be willing to step in at the last minute when another speaker fails to show. This will earn you a ton of brownie points. And you'll be remembered as the one who did the impossible.

- **Reciprocate.** Get to know the other lawyers and professionals who are speaking on similar topics. Recommend them when you can't accept a speaking engagement. Be generous.

- **Create your own opportunity.** Lawyers have been organizing seminars and workshops for potential clients for decades. An estates lawyer might work through the local recreation center or Lions Club to schedule a special program on how individuals draft their own wills—providing a venue for identifying complex will issues that require a lawyer. An employment lawyer could work with a corporate lawyer (inside your firm or not) to organize an afternoon program on emerging legal issues related to new tax laws.

CHAPTER

12

Leave Them Speechless When You Give a Speech

Standing next to a lectern in your best Sunday suit and speaking to a crowd through a microphone doesn't necessarily make you an effective public speaker. We've all suffered through presentations that should never have made the big time. And we've all walked away from one muttering about how the speaker not only failed to enchant us but, frankly, didn't seem to have a clue. Clearly, no one is going to call that speaker for advice.

> **If people wanted to read a book, they could stay home. Instead, challenge yourself to do your entire presentation with slides containing only photos. No words."**

Speaking engagements can work against you just as easily as they can help you. Getting the invitation to speak is the easy part. It's what you do with the invite that counts. Your goal? Make sure everyone in the audience knows you are knowledgeable about your subject and focused on solutions before you walk away with business cards and phone numbers from people who have more questions for you.

With a little advance thought (and don't you dare give a speech without advance thought!), it's fairly simple to put a speech together with information that represents you and your firm well. But it's how you present that information—and yourself—that will draw new business.

And that might take some practice.

How do you look? Wear something comfortable that makes you feel like a million bucks. Clean, pressed and all shined up. While muted or dark colors look professional, the addition of a little something really bright near your face keeps everyone's eyes on you. A tie, scarf, jacket or necklace in a bright and flattering color will make everyone feel good. Even you. Comb your hair, brush your teeth, fix your lipstick. People will be staring at you for an hour with nothing better to do than pick apart your grooming. Head them off at the pass.

How do your slides look? Hopefully, they are clean, simple, crisp and thought-provoking. Lots of visuals, few words. Use this background to add punch to your ideas, but please don't use slides that merely repeat the words you are saying. Or vice versa. If people wanted to read a book, they could stay home. Instead, challenge yourself to do your entire presentation with slides containing only photos. No words. People will hang on your words to explain the mystery of what you are showing them instead of reading ahead and losing interest. And receiving information simultaneously in two different forms (visual and verbal) will only serve to reinforce your audience's retention of it.

How do you sound? You need to sound like you know what you're talking about! If you don't, rehearse until you do. Speak at a regular pace. Use pauses for emphasis or to allow people to catch up with you. Let the suspense build when appropriate. Smile when you speak; it improves your tone and makes you look good. If people say they can't hear you, it may be a sign that you need a little voice coaching to learn to project from the gut instead of from just behind your back teeth. And, yes, use a microphone, even if it seems pompous. It's what professionals do. No one will know how wonderful you are if they can't hear you. And having to shout will only crank up your anxiety and discomfort. On the subject of things you may feel embarrassed about? Yes, do stand up. No, don't stand behind a podium. Request a microphone that will allow you to move.

Tell stories. You know it's just wrong to just say, "Hey, folks, I'm really great at what I do!" So how do you demonstrate your competence and experience? Tell stories about cases you have been involved with, clients you have helped, anything that will expand the points you are making in your speech while illustrating that you are successful, busy and well connected. Worried about confidentiality? There are ways to tell stories without identifying names and details.

How will they remember you? Your last slide should simply have your name and contact information. Leave it up there for the duration so people can write it down. In addition, provide something they can take away with them besides the requisite speaker handout—the more useful and intriguing, the better. A checklist, board game, questionnaire. Think viral. If it's an amazing and relevant tool or document, they will want to share it with others, so give them the link to your website or another place to download it.

Most importantly, love what you're doing and believe what you're saying! It will show. And they'll love you right back.

Leverage It to Multiply the Marketing Impact

Say you've been invited to speak at the annual meeting of a group of not-for-profits next month. Specifically, they want to know what, if anything, they should be worrying about related to your specialty—trademarks and brands, for example. Easy-peasy.

You do the research to get up to date on current developments, get a little help pulling together slides, and then pin on that name tag and hit the podium with enthusiasm. This is your area of expertise. You could do this in your sleep, right? Then, when you step away from the podium, you file your notes, toss your name tag and feel grateful that's done so you can get back to the "real work." *Stop right there.*

It's a huge waste to do the work to give a speech and just leave it at that. Here are things you can do that might just double or triple your speaking engagement's marketing impact.

Write and publish the article. You've done the research. You've created some good visuals. You've even tested your material before a crowd of potential clients who helped you punch it up by asking questions that revealed the hottest buttons for that crowd. All you need is an hour or two to turn those spoken words into a written piece—and find someone interested in publishing it. (Most editors are voracious consumers of good content that matches their readership. Placing a good article won't be difficult. In fact, the monthly publication produced by the group that just invited you to speak should be your first contact.)

Give the speech again somewhere else. Again, you've done the prep work, so why not identify another group interested in the same issues? There are a handful of ways to do this. First, check with the people who invited you to the first event and ask if they know of others. If you did a good job, they will be eager to recommend you. Next, consider how your speech might be tweaked to appeal to a slightly different audience. Would the chamber of commerce like you to speak to small business owners about the "Top 10 Intellectual Property Worries for Small Businesses"? And unless all of the other lawyers in your firm are IP lawyers, too, make sure to share an informal version of the speech with your colleagues over a box lunch. They need to know what their clients should be worrying about so they can cross-sell your services. (If they are all IP lawyers, share your slides and notes so they can make a similar speech, too.)

Blog about it. Even if it's not your own personal blog—perhaps it's the firm's, or the chamber's, or even a national blog for nonprofit leaders—don't miss the opportunity to share what you know and demonstrate your ability to make complex legal issues understandable. In case you're wondering, yes, this is different from the article you are writing for a publication. It's shorter and more colloquial; it's filled with bullets and lists. And you want to place a link in your blog post that will take a reader right to your firm bio and the online version of the bigger, more informative article, too.

Throw your own party. By now, you have a pocketful of business cards from people who saw you speak, who are interested in learning more and want to make a personal connection. Invite them to join you for a Friday afternoon wine and cheese networking event in your conference room. Don't give a speech (though you might ask someone else, one of your clients, perhaps, to say a few words). This is just some end-of-the-week conviviality and an opportunity for participants to share notes with others in their position. Make sure there's something they can take with them when they leave. Oh, wait ... you've printed out copies of that article you published (with your firm's logo and contact information), haven't you?

"Productize" it. Sure, someone can attend one of your speeches and read the article. But once you've called out the top 10 worries, does that give them the expertise to determine whether their organization is safe? Of course not. That's why they need your help. But nonprofits don't have a lot of money to toss around, so you need to package that help in a way they can afford. Perhaps you train a junior (and therefore less-expensive) lawyer or a senior paralegal to visit their office and conduct an IP inventory using the detailed checklist you have prepared—for a flat fee. If they pass the inventory test, they will sleep better at night. If they don't pass the test and serious issues are exposed ... *that's* when they need to hire you.

Now that speech was really worth the time and effort after all, wasn't it? And those five ideas are only the tip of the iceberg when it comes to leveraging the hard work you put into that speech.

CHAPTER

13

Advertising and Publicity

The idea of having someone or something else do the work of getting clients for you is very appealing. But the truth is, no one has yet invented a good way to sit back elegantly practicing law while clients are delivered to you without your involvement. So, while it is tempting to believe that late-night TV spots, Google display ads, directory listings or magazine tombstone ads will be *the* answer to your prayers for more clients, they won't be—no more than any other single marketing tactic will be.

The same is true of hiring a publicist to "get your name in the paper." Sure, it is possible to dump enough money into either advertising or publicity to buy yourself some fame—but there's no guarantee that kind of fame will bring you clients.

So let's look at how you *can* use advertising and publicity to your advantage. To start with, let's define terms.

> **Advertising** is appealing information about goods or services that uses paid placement in print or electronic media and openly identifies the advertiser and her relationship to the marketing activity.
>
> **Publicity** is designed to attract public interest, generally through information with news value that is issued as a means of gaining mention in the editorial segments of the media and not identified as related to any marketing effort. No money is paid to the publication for inclusion in editorial text, though frequently an unaffiliated publicist is hired to accomplish it.

If you are prepared to invest money in advertising or publicity, you'll want to do so on the following basis:

- **Integrated.** Don't invest in advertising or PR unless it fits with and amplifies your overall marketing plan, complementing and leveraging all of the other tactics you've decided are appropriate for your ideal client.

- **High quality**. Pay professionals—photographer, copywriter, designer, media buyer and the like—to help you produce and place your ads to your maximum benefit. Don't think you can get by with something amateurish. You can't, and it will stick in people's minds much longer than you'd think.

- **Well targeted.** One of the great things about advertising is that you will have the ability to understand exactly who will see and read about you. Any publication—print or digital—that sells advertising space will provide demographic information about the readership if you ask. Then you can match those demographics with the description of your ideal client that you prepared at the beginning of this book. DO NOT buy ads on the basis of getting to the most people. You want to get the most RIGHT people. So if you are choosing between a national general-interest newspaper with a readership of 1.7 million and a teachers' union publication with distribution to 30,000 local members to sell your employment legal services to educators, go with the latter. It will be a lot cheaper and every single person who sees the ad will already be a potential client for your services! Online, Google ads and social media ads via Facebook, Twitter and LinkedIn let you target keywords and specific demographics, too. Staunchly resist any temptation to advertise to other lawyers (e.g., in one of those Super-Duper Lawyer publications or a bar association magazine) unless you expect the majority of your work to come from other lawyers—if, say, your practice focuses on legal malpractice or something highly specialized, such as patent defense work.

- **Ethical.** Become familiar with the rules of professional conduct in the jurisdiction where you practice. Advertising set off a lot of warning bells 30 years ago and some bar associations haven't caught up with the changes. Do not inadvertently run afoul of your state's ethics committee.

- **Attention grabbing and unique.** The main reason to look at other lawyers' ads is to remind yourself what not to do. Advertising only works when it stands out from the crowd, knows what it is selling and speaks directly to the consumer. So don't copy others. Be different and express what is unique about you and your services. When assessing the impact of an ad campaign, the professionals consider both the "creative" (the images and words) and the "placement" (where it is printed, displayed or shown). It's a mistake to consider one without the other.

PART 3
Networking and Personal Sales

At this point, you know your mission statement, your target market and how you will assemble the unique services you wish to sell to your ideal clients. You've reviewed a menu of marketing tactics, considering how each would fit into a mix of activities designed to get you in front of that target market in a way that speaks persuasively to them.

Up to this point, we've been talking about marketing. In very general terms, marketing is to sales what plowing and fertilizing the back forty is to planting the year's seed corn. By the time you sit down face to face with potential clients, they should have been exposed sufficiently to your marketing information that they will be predisposed to hire you. So now let's get "personal." In this segment, you will:

1. Learn about right ways and wrong ways to **build your personal network** of contacts.

2. Draft an **"elevator speech"**—a way to quickly explain what you do and for whom. (It's that mission statement, really.)

3. Get guidance on **proposals, pitches and presentations**, both formal and informal.

4. Get ready to **receive (and give) referrals.**

GETTING CLIENTS **83**

CHAPTER

14

Networking

Every lawyer needs a good network. With fellow lawyers, yes. But you need lots of other people in your network as well. Remember that spreadsheet filled with contacts you started at the beginning of this book? You already have a network, even if you haven't thought of it that way.

A broad and growing network is important, and not just because it's a source of new business. Smart lawyers draw on (and give back to) their networks for ideas, introductions, information, collaboration, and plenty of other things critical to a healthy law practice.

The Networking Basics

Unfortunately, the mere term "networking" can be intimidating to the uninitiated, and off-putting even to seasoned professionals.

So let's adjust that attitude with a collection of important tips to guide you in continuing to develop your network. A network that works for everyone involved—not just for you.

- Pretending to like people you really can't stand on the off chance they will hire you is just bad form.

- You aren't going to be able to build a network without leaving the safety of your office and home.

- It is virtually impossible to build relationships with new people if you don't carry something like a business card that you can easily share.

- You need a good elevator speech. Make it memorable. (More on that later.)

- Never expect to receive before you give.

- You are here to help others (remember your mission?)—not to sell things to them.

- To truly hear what someone needs, you must be a good and conscientious listener.

- Be the host of the conversation. Put people at ease.

- Ask questions. Be genuinely interested. How else can you learn about a new person?

- You can meet people you want to add to your network anywhere. *Anywhere.*

> **"** Once you've focused in on the best activities, don't just introduce yourself. Introduce people to each other. (This is your chance to brag on someone!)"

- Most people think "marketing" when they think "networking." But building relationships with people is good for far more than just business development—although it doesn't hurt that, either.

- You need a good handshake. Make sure your forearm is roughly parallel to the floor, grip firmly (don't squeeze) and pump once … okay, maybe twice.

- Successful networking is a habit.

- Anyone will feel good about a conversation with you if you express interest in them. No need to flatter, just be interested.

- Smart networkers keep track of new information about people they know—what they do, who they know, birthdays, vacations. It improves your ability to help them.

- Smile.

- Hiring you will rarely be the immediate answer to the problems of people in your network. But by providing answers—an introduction, a referral, information, new perspective, an invitation, a tip—you can demonstrate that you are a source of useful answers and that you want to help.

- You can't attend every single networking event that might present opportunities. Develop your own criteria for selection—will your clients attend? Does it relate to your practice focus? Has someone with clout offered to make introductions?

NETWORKING AND PERSONAL SALES

> *Great networks don't happen by accident. Plan to meet the right people."*

- You never know who will end up changing your world.

- At events, a glass of soda water with lemon serves the same purpose as a cocktail while allowing you to keep your edge.

- Don't just introduce yourself. Introduce people to each other. (This is your chance to brag on someone!)

- It is smart to organize for networking: thank-you reminders, holiday card ticklers and so on. Remember to keep building your contact list.

- Even if you are wearing a name badge, say your name out loud when you meet a new person. Some people remember what they read. Some remember what they hear. And some names require help with pronunciation.

- Wear your name badge on the same side as your handshake hand—that way their eyes will rest easily on the badge.

- If you read something online that reminds you of someone in your network, copy the URL and email it to them with a note. At a loss for words? Try "This made me think of you!"

- Steer away from topics of conversation that others may find controversial—religion, sex, politics—unless you already know you come down on the same side or it relates directly to your practice focus.

- Either manage what you post on social media in such a way that you avoid offending, or get really, really good at managing your privacy settings.

- If it's an event where they're serving hors d'oeuvres, eat before you go. Then your hands will be available and goo-free for shaking.

- Learn to tell a good story.

- Help others achieve their goals. (Say thank you when they help you reach yours.)

- When out in public, carry your business cards in your right pocket. When presented with someone else's card, place it in your left pocket. That way you'll never get confused.

- It's easy to initiate a business card exchange: "Have you got a card? I'd like to follow up on this conversation later."

- Take care not to spread rumors—you never know who knows the person you may be gossiping about. Keep others' secrets to yourself.

- Great networks don't happen by accident. Plan to meet the right people.

- Body language speaks volumes. Keep your hands out of your pockets and don't fold your arms when you're socializing.

- Be nice.

Some Cautions

Meeting new people and networking comes naturally to some. To others—not so much. If you are one of the latter, here are a few more points to keep you focused.

The "Give First" rule is critical. You are networking to find people who could benefit from your professional assistance. That said, it is really, really important to remember to *give* something before you expect to receive. No one likes the jerk who, upon first meeting, says something like, "I'm a products liability lawyer. You should dump your current firm and give me all your work." However, we might respond really well to something along these lines: "My firm has a nifty new app that will run profit and loss numbers on all your outside legal service providers. Here, let me send you a link." In fact, down the line, you will probably be the first person that guy thinks of when he uses your app and finds out how much money he's losing with his current lawyer.

It's not a numbers game. Your goal isn't to get as many business cards into as many hands as possible. It is to identify people you can help who are well positioned to help you someday and to build relationships with them. You're looking for quality, not quantity. No one can be expected to build relationships (let alone productive relationships) with hundreds of people. But good relationships with a handful of the right people can work like magic for your career. Tip: Do your research in advance of attending events to figure out who you really want to meet, then make it happen.

Social media isn't the answer. Some really amazing relationships have been built and maintained online. But don't think, just because you're tweeting frequently, that you have built a network of those who follow you on Twitter. Most of them aren't reading your tweets; they are too busy tweeting themselves. It's going to take some in-person time, some on-the-telephone time and some personal just-between-us emails. Do your research, figure out who you can help who might help you, then make contact and invite them out for coffee or lunch and a good long talk. *That's* how you begin a working relationship.

CHAPTER 15

That Elevator Speech

The whole point of meeting new people is to learn whether there is the opportunity to build a relationship—relationships are the foundation of potential and continuing connections with clients. But to figure out if there is an opportunity, you're going to need a conversation.

Say we've just met:

> Hello, I'm Merrilyn Tarlton. When I'm not writing books like this one, I work with my partners to deliver "one really good idea every day" to help lawyers build careers and lives that they love.

If you are tempted to respond with a quick, "I'm Timothy Torts and I'm a lawyer," well, shame on you.

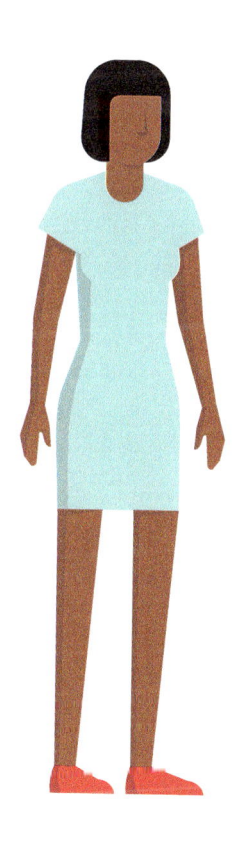

NETWORKING AND PERSONAL SALES **91**

When you introduce yourself, you need to give the other person a good handle on who you are. Something they can grab on to, remember and use to keep the conversation going.

There are few better ways to shut down a conversation than by saying, "Hi, I'm a lawyer." Period.

How about, instead of saying what you "are … ," you tell me what you do? Now aren't you glad you put the work into figuring out your personal mission statement? Perhaps you are a business lawyer who "advises owners about the sale of their businesses."

Maybe you "advise large energy corporations on compliance with federal statutes that protect the environment and the resources of tribal lands."

Here are a few more examples:

> "I work with aviation companies in their acquisition and operation of commercial aircraft."
>
> "I help private property owners navigate eminent domain, condemnation, takings and property rights proceedings."
>
> "I protect children's interests in complex divorce proceedings."

I think you get the idea: Who do you help and what do you help them do? Now it's just a simple matter of putting together your own introductory sentence. Bear in mind that you may want to modify its emphasis to speak best to the people you are meeting. Give them something really interesting and they will respond with a question, and then you're off to the races with a good conversation that will ideally result in:

- The two of you getting to know and understand each other a bit.
- This new contact having a clearer idea about what you do and how you can help.
- You knowing what this new person does, the kind of people he knows and what problem he would love help solving.

If you believe you could help them with something, give them your card (at least) and offer to meet for coffee or a chat to explore the possibilities. If their problem isn't in your wheelhouse but you know someone who might be able to help them, offer to contact them later to facilitate that connection. Even then, you will be remembered as a source of solutions and help.

CHAPTER 16

Proposals: Give Them Something to Say Yes To

It started in the construction-related professions long before it hit the business of law —corporate or government clients issuing a request for proposal or request for qualifications as an invitation for contractors, manufacturers and other vendors to express interest, prove their fitness for the work specified and bid competitively on the contract.

There is a lot of good material on how to play to win in this high-stakes game that has now spread to the legal profession. A web search will yield materials on the topic from a variety of resources (e.g., LexisNexis, the National Law Review, Lex Mundi, Law 360 and more). If you are interested in developing client relationships

> **In essence, you are drawing her a picture and putting a price on it. Giving her something to say yes to."**

with large organizations or government entities, educate yourself fully to prepare to toss your hat into the ring. Large law firms that compete for work in this way often employ dedicated technical, sales and writing staff to support their high-net-worth efforts.

The concept of providing a proposal to do legal work, however, can be scaled to any situation. It's a safe assumption, for example, that anyone seeking legal help will be concerned about how much the services will cost, and, nearly as universally, how the process will work. You can create a simple proposal letter that makes that information crystal clear. Do this well, and it should be an easy matter for them to say yes to your offer of help.

For example, let's say one of your contacts is planning to leave her long-time employer and start a competing business in partnership with a colleague. And let's assume the legal aspects of that maneuver are right up your alley. Unless this contact is a lawyer herself (and perhaps not even then), she will have only a sketchy idea of why she needs a lawyer's help. It is also likely that she will have some dread about the possibility of high legal fees. What a great opportunity for you to say: "Let me put something in writing for you. Let me show you how I can help—and how easy the process can be."

By the end of a short informational interview with her, you should have enough information to write a simple letter or email listing the work that you anticipate will be necessary and indicating how you will set your fees for it. With the letter, include background information that demonstrates you are highly qualified and experienced with this type of business transaction.

The beauty of this is that you don't have to rely on her ability to envision what she needs, how you will provide it, or the possible booby-traps and scope of your fees. And she doesn't have to pretend that she already knows all about it out of fear of appearing uninformed. In essence, you are drawing her a picture and putting a price on it. Giving her something to say *yes* to.

Your proposal letter will be structured simply, addressing five elements:

1. **What.** A description of the circumstances requiring legal assistance as you understand them.

2. **Scope.** A list of the services that will be necessary. Be as specific as possible. Don't say "meetings to discuss"; specify "four weekly meetings." Don't say "reviews and revisions of agreement"; put "review and modify the agreement up to three times." Spell out exactly what you intend to do and what you expect the client to do. You'll see why in a moment.

3. **Time frame.** An estimated timeline for the delivery of those services.

4. **Plan.** An explanation of how you will work together, including what will happen if or when circumstances change.

5. **Fee.** The fee to perform the services described. DON'T PANIC: Many lawyers are afraid of giving a fee estimate up-front out of concern that they can't anticipate all possible developments and will cheat themselves if the project spins out of control. Simple solution: When quoting anything other than a strict hourly rate for actual hours, specify that the fee will necessarily change if and when the scope of work changes. (That's why the emphasis on being specific about scope in No. 2, above.) So if part way into the matter, a new development forces you to go back and revise a strategy, you can communicate with the client concerning the

additional work (and time) this will entail and she should be prepared for changes to the original fee estimate.

This written proposal can be as brief as a single page letter or as comprehensive as a 200-page bound booklet, depending on what is required by the client or the nature of the project.

Whatever the size, once your proposal is in writing, schedule an in-person meeting to discuss it, preferably at the same time that you present it in writing. At this point, you will have shown that you understand and communicate well, conveyed that you have the experience and capability to do the job, and illustrated your respect for the prospective client's time, concerns and wallet.

Who could resist you?

CHAPTER
17

Pitches and Presentations

You may at times be given the opportunity to present the details of your proposal to a group in a more formal competition—against other lawyers doing the same. In this kind of structured competition, the parameters are generally dictated by the potential client in advance. If the specifics aren't laid out, call and ask! That's not cheating, it's just smart business practice.

A smart lawyer always does her research, learning as much as possible about the situation from the potential client, personal contacts, lawyers who represented this client previously, the internet, media reports—scour every possible source. There are few things more

NETWORKING AND PERSONAL SALES **99**

> **❝** And if you think your superior capabilities will override any gender issues, get over yourself. There may be someone on the other side whose capabilities match yours, leaving only gender to break the tie."

powerful in a competition selection process than a participant who knows what she is talking about.

Beyond that, here are a few guidelines for in-person presentations to potential clients.

They are the focus. This is about what the client needs. It is not all about you. Spend the briefest time possible talking about your qualifications and experience in the type of matter at hand, then focus on what they need and how you are going to solve their problem. Keep your vast qualifications and impressive honors inside the written materials package you've already given to the client.

Be strategic about who makes the presentation. If this is a big, complex legal project, you may be tempted to show off your firm's "depth and breadth" by assembling many of the firm's lawyers for the presentation. Don't. Even if it's a complex deal, the client is interested in knowing only the very small number of people they will deal with directly, and whether those people have the needed management chops and will be easy to work with.

(True story: A major regional law firm was invited to present to a team of lawyers setting up relationships around the country to handle an expected tsunami of plaintiffs' personal injury cases. This firm decided it could blow the competition out of the water by parading all 81 of its amazing litigators past a microphone to share their individual credentials before the committee. The selection committee got up and left before they were halfway through this vanity show.)

Difference matters. Think carefully about the optics of your presentation team—ethnic and gender diversity do count. Find out ahead of time about the group to whom you will be presenting. Even if it's a bunch of old white guys, they will probably have organizational diversity concerns. And if you think superior capabilities will override any gender issues, you are wrong. There may be someone on the other side whose capabilities match yours, leaving only gender to break the tie.

Practice, practice, practice. If you appear to approach this presentation casually, the selection group will expect you to take the work casually—and no one wants to pay good money for that. So, with ample time to change course, practice your presentation before a group of informed volunteers. Then invite questions. Ask what they liked about the presentation. Ask what they didn't. Modify and do it again.

Use visuals expertly. PowerPoint, Keynote, Prezi or handheld poster boards—make them as simple as possible (no swooping titles and bouncing bullets, please!) and use them to illustrate critical or potentially confusing points that need to be made. Do not use them as a prompt for yourself and especially DO NOT READ FROM YOUR SLIDES. You are demonstrating that you know this stuff, not that you know how to read, correct? Call ahead to make certain there are no barriers—room configuration, large windows, screens—to your masterful use of your presentation technology. Above all, use your visuals to demonstrate how expertly you can simplify complexity.

Be a strong presenter. Stand up. Dress well. Speak clearly. Look people in the eyes when you speak. "Host" their experience by checking for understanding, inviting questions and responding comfortably.

Smile. You like these people. Let them like you. Look forward to enjoying working together.

You know how to do this. You practiced trial presentation in law school, and if you've ever been to court, you know what to do to get your case across. This is merely a presentation to convince a prospect.

You've got this!

CHAPTER 18

Laying the Groundwork for Referrals

Before getting into the "how-tos" of obtaining referrals, you'd best take a hard look at whether you are referrable.

If you're like most people, when you move to a new town, you ask around for a good doctor or dentist. Well, in one fashion or another, that's how people find lawyers as well. Even now, when lawyer advertising is *everywhere,* a personal recommendation from someone whose opinion you trust trumps a late-night TV commercial or online listing every time.

So, before you can expect anyone to share your phone number with their friends or colleagues, you are going to need to show how they can wow their friends by sending them to you.

Of course, do good work. Remember that, unless they went to law school, your clients aren't really equipped to judge the quality of a brief, the soundness of a strategy or the tightness of a contract. So they are going to judge the quality of your work on the basis of things they do know about: clear and easy communications, speed, availability, attitude, helpfulness, collaboration, maybe even how easy it is to find a parking space near your office. So while it certainly helps to win the big case, the experience of working with you counts for a lot, too.

Make it enjoyable. Often a lawyer's work involves near life-or-death seriousness. But that doesn't mean a visit to your office has to be a somber one. People who feel cared about, advocated for and respected will always think well of you. Rule of thumb: People value most those who see them as they see themselves. And it doesn't always take an in-person meeting to express a level of caring, either. There are good ways to communicate warmly, even when it is electronic. Know people's names and the names of those close to them. Remember key dates. Go the extra mile to see that their needs are taken care of—whether it's a simple glass of water or introductions to others who can help with issues they face.

Be on time and on dollar. Demonstrate how you meet deadlines and conform to budgets. Communicate flawlessly about money, regularly. Value your client's time as well as your own.

Be trustworthy. If you say you are going to do something, do it.

Be honest. To a fault. Even when the news is difficult, don't sugarcoat it. Don't put off delivering it.

Solve problems, don't make them. Instead of saying, "No, you can't do that," try saying, "Well, here's what we'll need to do so you can do that." It's a simple wording change, but it means a lot when you take on something tough.

See things from the client's side of the table. People hire lawyers to serve on their team, not to tell them what they can and cannot do. Good team members learn everything they can about the work of the team, exchange "atta boys" with one another, understand where everyone is coming from, share the agony of defeat and the euphoria of victory. Find out how to conform with their billing needs, technology requirements and the like—make it clear that you are there to serve *their* needs.

Manage the entire experience. This includes welcome, thank-you and engagement letters. Clear communication about bills. Promptly answered phone calls and emails. Involve your assistant, receptionist and other staff members in building the relationship and making the client feel important. Make parking easy. Remove potentially offensive reading material from your reception area. Provide Wi-Fi and a quiet corner to visitors. If you will meet in your office, make sure it's tidy. If it's impossibly untidy, do not meet there.

If a lot of this sounds like window dressing, then know that perception is more than half of a satisfied client's experience. (Remember, too, that studies repeatedly show that when a client relationship focused on delicate legal problems is aggravated by poor client service, sketchy communications or simply a perception of something less than care, it is more likely to end in malpractice litigation.)

You Need to Ask for It, Too!

Don't think you can just do all this wonderful stuff and referred clients will beat a path to your door. You've got to ask for what you want in this world. If you send a message—by actions or words—that you are terribly busy or ... ahem ... far too exceptional at what you do to actually accept new clients, no one is going to refer friends or colleagues to you.

You need to take a more proactive posture. Make sure your clients and contacts know that you are always interested in referrals, and find opportunities to ask for introductions and referrals. One of the best ways to do this is during a routine post-engagement review of the work that has been accomplished for a client.

At the successful close of any significant matter, schedule a time to meet and review what was done and what was learned. A continuing client, pleased with the work you have done, will agree to do this as an investment in an ongoing and improved working relationship. As you reflect together on the matter and your client is reminded how well everything went and how much she enjoys working with you (don't neglect to find out what you might have done better, too!), you can gracefully ask if she might know other parties with similar challenges and if she would be willing to make an introduction.

Other Referral Sources

Referrals don't just come from clients. They can come from anyone with good knowledge of you and your practice. So when you become active in a trade association or community organization, remember that when observing how you get things done on that program committee, people file away knowledge that you are an effective and intelligent individual—clearly a good lawyer!

Also, share information with your friends, colleagues and contacts about the kind of law you practice and tell stories that illustrate specifically what you've done for clients. Your name will be at the top of their mind when someone they know says they have just such a problem and are looking for just such a lawyer.

CHAPTER 19

Cross-Selling

Many lawyers express discomfort about personally selling their services, feeling there is something inappropriate in "bragging" about one's abilities. I have two things to say about that. One, get over it. Two, get into cross-selling.

Cross-selling is about promoting the services of someone else. If you are in a big firm with a variety of different service offerings, it is a simple matter to introduce one of your colleagues to someone you know who is a potential client for them. Not only is it easy to brag about someone else, it makes you look good because you know great resources and your colleague ends up liking and wanting to help you, too.

Why Won't My Colleague Cross-Sell Me?

Well, really ... why should he? I mean, knowing that people do things for their own reasons and not for yours, what's in it for your partner to cross-sell you? Why should he introduce you to his client and promote you as someone who could help with a particular issue? Okay, I suppose there are several reasons you might suggest.

- **It's the right thing to do.** Says who? You think it's the right thing to do because you stand to gain by it. But does he? Maybe. Maybe not. Maybe he thinks (or thinks he knows!) that you're not really very good at what you do. Or that you have a history of acting badly when it comes to clients. Or that you're a mediocre lawyer. Perhaps none of those things are true, but does he know they aren't?

- **It's the best thing for his client.** We'll assume your partner wants to do the absolute best by this client. If he does, he'll find the absolute best person to help. Maybe that's you. Maybe it isn't. (See above for what he does and does not know.) Regardless, if there is a lawyer in another firm with a stellar national reputation, she would be the safe bet. Right?

- **It's what you'd do.** Is it? *Really?* Then you must do it all the time already. If you don't, you should examine why you don't. (You'll learn a lot.) If you really do cross-sell, maybe you do have the right to feel that you are owed. But only a jerk would expect to be handed a client just because he's owed. (See above for what's best for the client.)

- **That's what partners do.** Not really. Partners share expenses and profits. Good partners provide emotional and intellectual support. They grow their business together. They demand and give the best of each other. They tell the truth. And they're loyal. But they don't sacrifice their clients for each other. (See above for what they do and do not know.)

> *If you really do cross-sell, maybe you do have the right to feel that you are owed. But only a jerk would expect to be handed a client just because he's owed."*

Get the Message?

Until your partner knows you are the right and best lawyer for the job, you won't be cross-sold. (Unless your partner is nuts. But that's another conversation altogether.) It's your job to make sure each of your partners knows you've absolutely got the right stuff to help their clients or contacts in a way that makes them—the lawyer—look good.

I know it seems weird to think in terms of marketing to your own partner. But for a smart lawyer, it is marketing job No. 1. Though it may be your most challenging marketing task of all.

Here are a few things you can do inside your firm.

- **Make sure others know what it is that you do.** Don't be one of those boring people who drone on and on about themselves. But do share stories about what you're working on. Describe the challenges. Share the outcomes. Don't forget to ask others what they are up to as well.

- **Publicize victories.** If you're in a largish firm, there are probably already institutional ways to do this—an internal newsletter, intranet, internal blog. If not, find a way to do it in group meetings or casually over lunch. Maybe you could introduce a "what's new" beginning to regular meetings during which everyone can share news, good and bad. Again, beware of boasting. But you're a grown-up, you know how to do this. At a minimum, you can tell about someone else's victories, awards or promotions. Before long, they'll be telling others about yours.

NETWORKING AND PERSONAL SALES

- **Organize training sessions over internal lunches.** Get your firm's trusts and estates people to make a presentation about what your clients should know about estate planning—arming everyone with ways to help their clients informally. Follow up next month with something from the trial lawyers about how to assess a contingency fee case when choosing whether to take it on. The next month, a patent lawyer talks about the growing value of ideas in mergers and acquisitions. You get the picture. Educate one another and, in the process, you'll grow to respect and admire one another.

- **Invite a colleague to join you for lunch with one of your important clients.** Ask the right questions. Guide the conversation in the right way, and your client will be moved to tell your partner how great you are and what you did for her lately. And, oh yes, you'll be modeling the confidence you hope he'll have to introduce you to one of his important clients.

- **Make him look like a hero.** Let's say there's new law in your area of focus that you anticipate will affect a partner's client. Put something simple in writing, like a cheat sheet, to help him speak knowledgeably about it to the client. Or maybe it's a simple fact sheet that he can hand to the client. Both come with the expectation that "for more information" you will be brought in.

There's more—so much more—you can do to help your colleagues help you. Goodness knows, they can't do it without you.

THE MARKETING EMERGENCY

I know, I know ... you've come this far in the book, but what you still really need is clients **right now!**

IT CAN BE FRUSTRATING, BUT IT'S TRUE ...

Effective business **development**, the kind **that sets** you up for a successful career that you enjoy and profit **from**, is a long-term proposition. There is no switch you can just **flip**, no pill you can just pop that will make the clients beat a pathway to your office door.

That said, there can be times when things are so slow you literally don't know where your next dollar will come from and, even if actual starvation isn't a real possibility, the mortification of your **partners'** disapproving **sidelong** glances comes close to immobilizing you. While you understand and buy into the long-term approach, you also need to do something NOW, right?

There are things you can do that will produce work in the short term. Here are a few to keep your head above water while you get the ball rolling.

Talk to people. Remember the complete list of contacts you made at the beginning of this book? Well, pull that list up on your screen right now and start making phone calls! Set up times for lunches, coffee meetings, a drink after work, a ballgame or the like—with as many contacts as makes sense. On your dime. Say your purpose is to "catch up," "check in" or pick their brains about a topic of interest to you in your work. (The last one is particularly good, since it communicates that you respect them as experts.) During your in-person conversations, ask about family and friends, probe to learn how things are with this person, what's new in her life or business, and what's keeping her up nights. Part of your goal is to get to know your contacts and their needs better should your help be required in the future. Part of the goal is to remind them by your presence that you are interested in and available to work with them. Another part of your goal is to learn if they know others to whom they'd be willing to introduce you.

Take advantage of your unique expertise. Often, things you've learned in your recent work can lead to ideas about new kinds of services you can provide to clients. Perhaps you handled a case involving unnecessary liability created when information meant to be held in confidence was shared by mistake. How might you help other clients avoid these types of problems? How about an in-house lunchtime employee training session on the proper handling of information via email and letters, in elevators, etc. Develop the program up-front and sell it at a flat rate to different client organizations. There are lots of ways you might configure this sort of preventative consultation: an intellectual property audit, employee handbook review, estate planning assistance for the organization's employees, etc.

Why do you pay dues, anyway? Check to make certain that your name and practice are included in the referral system of all bar associations to which you belong. Check into bar referral services in your jurisdiction via the Online ABA Lawyer Referral Directory of state and local bar associations.

It's worth a shot! If you've got a bit of time on your hands—and if you're desperate for clients, you do—spend time looking into online referrals from organizations like Avvo and Rocket Lawyer.

Get out there and mix. Participate in things. Your bar association is probably organized by area of law. Sure, you should go to the monthly luncheon of the group that focuses on your field. But you should also participate with a complementary group or two. You're a patent lawyer? Find out when the business law group gathers and join in—these are people whose clients need your services.

Don't forget your colleagues are your clients as well. If, for example, you've developed a system of review that quickly identifies potential risk in a company's document retention policies, make sure your partners and other professional connections know about it. Introducing you to their clients could benefit everyone.

WARNING: Your chances of making something happen by applying these techniques are quite high. So go ahead and jump on it, but don't allow yourself to become distracted to the point that you forget about consciously and systematically building your long-term business development strategy, too. Because if you forget that, you'll soon find yourself right smack up against another one of these marketing emergencies. And even if you don't, it will be because you are doing work other than the kind you really want to do.

PART 4
Getting It Done

Now you know what you want to do and who you want to do it for and have a pretty good understanding of your options for getting out in front of them. That means it's time to get down to work.

In this segment, you will:

1. Draft a **simple marketing plan**.
2. Learn a **project management technique** to help you get it done.
3. Figure out how you want to **track your progress**.
4. Put things in place to **keep yourself motivated** and working your plan.

CHAPTER 20

Your Marketing Plan Worksheet

Now it's time to take what you've learned in this book and put it to work building your dream law practice. On the following pages are a series of simple forms to be completed by you. When you are done, they will add up to a basic marketing plan. Choose wisely and avoid selecting *everything* possible. Doing a few of the right things really well is so much more effective than trying to do everything and being successful at none of it.

GETTING IT DONE 117

First your basic mission:

PERSONAL MISSION STATEMENT:	
So that:	(who)
Can:	(do what)
I will:	(help by)

Now, how will you tell people what you do?

ELEVATOR SPEECH:

How will you get ready to deliver your services? For example:

THINGS I WILL NEED TO DO TO ADDRESS THE UNIQUE MARKET AND ISSUES:	
Educate myself by:	
Find existing or new staff resources to:	
Get technology that will:	
Locate my office(s):	
Package my services:	
Price my services:	

Next, putting the marketing pieces together:

We've explored a good number of marketing and business development tactics in this book. Not all will apply to your specific market. Select the ones that do and fill in the blanks with specific answers targeting your exact potential clients. If a particular tactic isn't right for your market, leave the space empty and move on.

I WILL BECOME KNOWN BY:	
Speaking on:	
Writing and publishing about:	
Joining and participating in:	
Giving to:	
Collaborating with:	
Advertising via:	
Pursuing publicity by:	
Starting a new organization for:	
Other:	

Here, select the media channels most appropriate for your target market and describe how you will use those channels to reach the right people.

I WILL SHARE MY CONTENT THROUGH THESE CHANNELS:	
Blog:	
Social Media:	
LinkedIn	
Twitter	
Facebook	
Other	
Video:	
Podcasts:	
Email Marketing:	
Content Syndicators:	
Book:	
Newsletter:	
Trade/Industry Publications:	
Other:	

Naturally, you will need electronic and print means of communicating with people about your practice. Chances are you will require almost all of the items listed here. Make sure you include the specific ways in which your materials will be tailored to appeal to your target market.

I WILL CREATE THESE MARKETING MATERIALS:	
Website:	
Personal Biography (with professional photo):	
Business Cards:	
Letterhead:	
Email Signature Block:	
Social Media Accounts:	
Brochure:	
Case Studies:	
Checklists:	
Reprints:	
Other:	

Keep Your Assets Up to Date

At the beginning of the book, we looked at the basic kinds of information you will collect and manage over time so you can draw on them as needed—confident that they are current. You will want to include in your marketing plan the important time necessary to keep on top of this.

I WILL CREATE AND MAINTAIN:	
Personal Contact List:	
Resume Database:	
Other:	Personal biography(ies) and photo(s)
	Online directory listings
	Record of positive client feedback

CHAPTER
21

Project Managing Your Marketing Plan

Okay, it's time to get to work on that plan. But jumping in anywhere isn't the best way. A bit of time laying out your plan in more detail can create a system of project management to keep you on the right track, helping to ensure the work actually gets done and preventing that feeling of "overwhelm" that can come on so quickly.

Here's a simple way to approach project management. It will consume some time up-front, so you may choose to set aside a day to get it all done. It will be worth it.

1. **Make a list.** List all of the tasks that you identified in your Marketing Plan Worksheet.

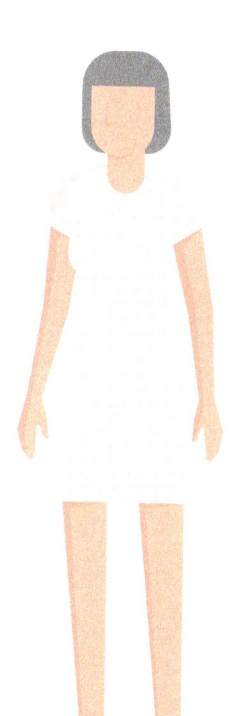

2. **Order them.** You know right out of the box that some things will need to be done before others. If you're getting new business cards, that's going to happen before you go to a networking lunch, right?

3. **Do your research.** Let's say one of the tasks you identified was "Attend the annual meeting of the National Music Publishers Association." You'll need to do some research to learn when and where the meeting will be held this year, the deadline for registration, whether you must be a member, and so on.

4. **Keep breaking it down.** Break each one of your tasks into subtasks in the order they must be done. For the example above, it will look something like this:

    ☐ **Attend NMPA Annual Meeting, 6/23**

    ☐ Register

    ☐ Make hotel and travel arrangements

    ☐ Pack business cards and materials

    ☐ Attend meeting

    ☐ Record notes, contacts and follow up upon return

5. **Assign a date by which each of those items will be done.** Do this for all of your tasks.

6. **Create a spreadsheet.** (Don't try to do this with pen and paper! You'll hate yourself after the first five minutes. You're going to need to do a lot of moving things around.) Across the top, label columns with the first date of each week going forward: 6/6, 6/13, 6/20, etc. Down the left side, list your tasks in order, including their subtasks right beneath them. At this point, it will look something like this:

PROJECT/TASK	WEEK OF 6/6	WEEK OF 6/13	WEEK OF 6/20	WEEK OF 6/27
Business Cards:				
Write text				
Order from printer				
Pick up cards				
NMPA Annual Meeting:				
Register				
Hotel/travel				
Pack				
Attend meeting				
Notes recorded				
Contacts preserved				
Weekly Business Development Lunch:				
Scheduling calls or emails				
Lunch				
Blog:				
Name/create blog				
Photos/graphics				
Write profile				
Write new post				

7. **Schedule your time.** Now you can just start placing an *x* in the boxes for the week when you plan to complete tasks. You'll find you need to do some adjusting as you work through this. Be mindful of those weeks that start to fill up, and move things forward or back to make sure you don't overwhelm yourself all in one week. It will start to look like this:

PROJECT/TASK	WEEK OF 6/6	WEEK OF 6/13	WEEK OF 6/20	WEEK OF 6/27
Business Cards:				
Write text	x			
Order from printer	x			
Pick up cards			x	
NMPA Annual Meeting:				
Register	x			
Hotel/travel	x			
Pack			x	
Attend meeting			x	
Notes recorded				x
Contacts preserved				x
Weekly Business Development Lunch:				
Scheduling calls or emails	x		x	
Lunches		x		x

8. **Make your weekly lists.** Based on the preceding chart (reading down from the top), my business development to-do list for the week of June 6 will include:

- ☐ Writing business card text
- ☐ Ordering business cards
- ☐ Registering for the NMPA Annual Meeting
- ☐ Making hotel and travel arrangements for NMPA
- ☐ Sending email or phone invitations for upcoming lunches

Your Constant Companion

It would be naive to assume that this planning stage is a once a year gig. The spreadsheet you've just created should be your constant companion. Check it at the end of each week to allow yourself the pleasure of crossing off those things you've accomplished and at the beginning of each week to freshen up your to-do list. Over time, add more columns with dates and develop new plans based on what you learn. As with all planning actions, things will happen that change the way your original plan looked—just go back in there and modify what you've done and keep on working the plan!

This way you can feel confident that your business development activity is always tied back to the overall goals that you set at the beginning of this book. And by breaking it into small tasks before you schedule it, you'll see it's not too difficult to fit marketing into your schedule.

This method of organizing your to-do list is only one of many. But it's a good, simple one that has worked for many people. Of course, if you are comfortable with productivity or project management apps, you can deploy them to help you stay on track, too. But don't get distracted by shiny tools and spend more time planning than doing. (It happens.)

GETTING REALLY CREATIVE

A word about precedent. Yes, under the doctrine of stare decisis, common-law judges are obliged to adhere to the precedents set by previously decided cases, where the facts are substantially the same. And your law career will largely focus in that direction. But good marketing practice is actually the reverse. Effective marketing differentiates you and your service or product so clearly that your potential client doesn't even need to make a choice—it will be obvious that you are the only lawyer he needs. So looking to what other lawyers have done can be a self-defeating exercise.

(I learned this the hard way when I moved from inside an advertising agency to inside a big law firm. For a while, working incredibly hard to develop strongly different and differentiating marketing ideas, I couldn't figure out why all the lawyers I worked with wanted to know was, "Has anyone else ever done this?" Very frustrating.)

In other words, "thinking like a lawyer" isn't going to be the best approach to your marketing and business development activities. Fortunately, you are pretty darn smart and capable of switching thinking-style gears when you need to. And here's a little help in thinking creatively—some warm-up exercises, if you will.

The Idea Generator

(WARNING! These exercises are guaranteed to produce interesting ideas. Some good, and some really, really bad. The quality of the idea—and its ability to transform your practice—rests with you.)

Cancel the meetings. Asking a creative person to produce a good idea in a large meeting is like putting a comedian on the spot by insisting, "Say something funny!" Go have a latte instead. Draw on napkins. Make paper airplanes.

Crank up the stimuli. Thumb through a magazine backward or upside down. Randomly pick out words from the dictionary. Go for a walk.

Decorate your office walls with pictures of what you want "it" to look like once you have your solution. Experience "it." (Call your office and pretend to be a client. Hire your competitor and see what being a client feels like.)

Take it apart and put it back together again. Remember the kid's activity books that reduced you to giggles when you created funny face after funny face by flipping new eyes, lips and noses into place? Do that with your business development challenge by experimenting with changing every single aspect of it one by one. Then see what you get.

Make hamburgers of sacred cows. Determine which parts of your tough nut are ironclad, carved in stone and unchangeable. Then change them. Or play with changing them just to see what happens.

Find fresher minds. Give your 8-year-old and his friends some chocolate milk, paper and markers. Describe your problem to them. Ask them what *they'd* do in response. Nine times out of 10, they'll go straight to the heart of the matter.

Behave like a kid yourself. Daydream. Draw pictures. Pass notes—sharing ideas leads to collaboration. Set up a flip chart in your office and scribble on it whenever the spirit moves. Leave it there. (Add. Refine. Toss. Frame.)

Look at it upside down. Think this doesn't work? Next time you do a crossword puzzle switch it around halfway through and see if you don't find seemingly unfindable answers when you are reading it upside down. Looking at things from different perspectives raises brand-new paradigms.

Okay, steal others' ideas. But not other lawyers' ideas. Learn how tech startups handle product roll out. How does an ad agency pitch new work? That hot-dog seller that's got 'em lined up down the street? Find out how her business practices might inspire yours.

CHAPTER

22

Keeping Track of Your Progress

The flip side of planning your marketing activities is measuring and keeping track of how you're doing along the way. Sure, you should pat yourself on the back as you cross things off your to-do list. You should feel good about accomplishing things you set out to do. But it's important to remember that, in this case, it's more about the destination than the journey. Are the things that you are doing working? If they aren't, how should you change them?

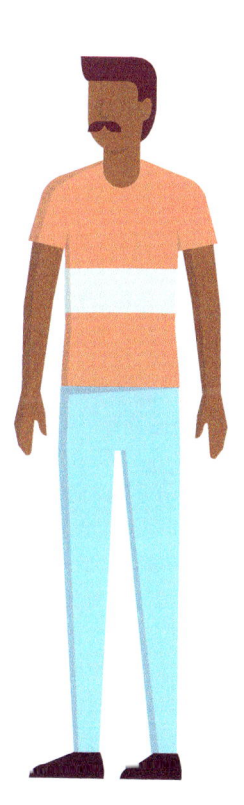

> **Do not let a month pass without identifying the total number of those clients with whom you are working and placing that number somewhere visible—on your iPad's home screen, your PC desktop, a chart on your wall. The more frequently in your line of sight, the better."**

The first step is to figure out what will indicate success for you. What have you set out to do? At the beginning of this book, you developed a statement focusing in on the type of work you want to do and the kind of people or organizations for whom you want to do it—your target market. That's a good starting place.

Ask yourself:

- Are you getting more of that sort of work?
- How will you gauge it? Time? Money? Number of clients? Number of inquiries? Number of inquiries turned into clients?

It's for you to decide which things will be most meaningful to track in the context of your practice and your market. But, whatever it is, make sure that the metrics you use to measure your progress relate directly to your marketing activities.

For example, if you have decided that you want your practice to focus on estate planning for young technology entrepreneurs, you probably want to keep track of how many estate planning gigs you get for that type of client each month. A simple number. Over time, if your plan is working, that number should go up. Do not let a month pass without identifying the total number of those clients with whom you are working and placing that number somewhere visible—on your

NEW CLIENTS BY MONTH

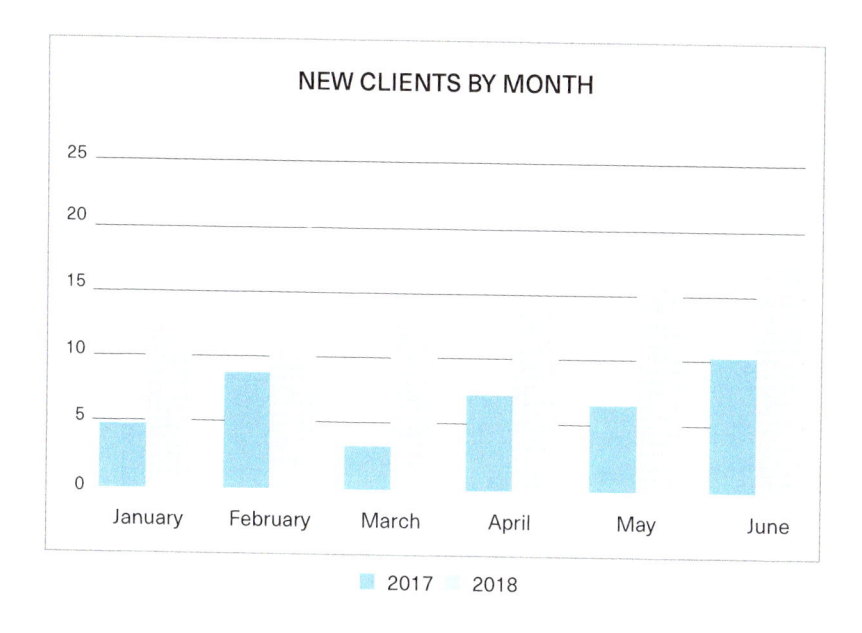

■ 2017 ■ 2018

iPad's home screen, your PC desktop, a chart on your wall. The more frequently in your line of sight, the better.

Of course, you also want to routinely record the number on a month-by-month basis in a spreadsheet or similar tool. By keeping track of that monthly number, you will be able to create a simple bar chart that allows you to enjoy the gradual sloping up in response to your hard work.

Perhaps you'll choose to measure the number of hours you spent doing that kind of work instead of (or in addition to) number of clients. Or, you could just keep track of only the new clients who engage you for these estate planning gigs each month. Obviously, there are a number of ways to keep an eye on this ball. Decide up-front what you're going to watch and then set up a system to easily retrieve that number once a month—as well as in an ongoing way. A graph or bar chart (like the one on the previous page) will work great.

Setting Goals

As you implement your new marketing plan and begin to see results, you'll learn what is reasonable to expect in terms of results. That's when you can begin to identify and set specific goals for yourself. Make them a bit of a stretch and work hard to reach them. Share these goals with important people in your life, so they can keep you honest about the progress you make. Having something to shoot for—and pleasing people you care about—is a great motivator.

CHAPTER 23

Staying Motivated

You may be all fired up and ready to go right now. But it can be challenging to keep that head of steam and overcome the natural human tendency toward procrastination. Nothing's going to happen unless you make it happen. So, here are a few tricks to keep the fire going.

Reward yourself. One would think that successful business development could be its own reward, but when you're up to your eyeballs in legal work it feels more like punishment than reward to keep ticking off the marketing to-dos on your list. So, right up-front, identify a goal and a reward that you will give yourself when you meet the goal. And don't let yourself get away with not taking the reward!

GETTING IT DONE

Ideas for rewards? Time off and travel are always good. Or something you've been wanting to buy for your office, home, car or family. Maybe it's something that doesn't require dollars, like time with your family or a day all to yourself to do just as you please. Go on, no one knows better than you what will motivate you.

Get a helpmate. There are lots of other lawyers in your world attempting to do just what you're trying to do. Find one you like and invite him to team up with you to keep motivated. Meet regularly—over coffee, lunch, racquetball, your kids' play group, whatever—and share your plans and to-do lists. Commit to deadlines. Debrief when it's over. If you're remotely competitive (and, having graduated from law school, who isn't?), you won't want to have to say, "I didn't get it done." Use that need to succeed in making progress with your marketing. (Of course, you'll want to select a helpmate who isn't a head-to-head competitor in your area, lest you feel the need to hold your plans too close to the vest.)

Form a support group. If you are in a larger firm, try pulling together a group of other lawyers who are at a similar point in their careers. In a small firm? Maybe your former law school classmates would be interested in cheering on one another and, subliminally, serving as a time clock on those critical marketing to-dos. Some lawyers have even created support groups with other, non-lawyer professionals—and managed, over time, to turn the group into a good source of referrals.

Make it simple. Break the big tasks down into little pieces. Then set the list of big things to one side and select only three little things at one time. It's way too easy to be overwhelmed by the size of a looming chore. Getting little things done is worth celebrating, too!

Consider a personal board of directors. What if you could assemble a group of high-level executives to advise on your career moves on a quarterly or semiannual basis? Well, you can. One solo lawyer I know created a "board of directors" consisting of his wife, father, mother and oldest child. Building a solo practice was a high-risk venture for him and he felt he needed to make absolutely certain he did everything necessary to make it work. So he developed a strategic plan and presented it to his family group. You can bet he pedaled like crazy to avoid having to sit down with this august (and invested!) group and report he wasn't doing what he'd promised. Other lawyers have invited a group of diverse professionals—accountant, marketing consultant, CEO, venture capitalist, etc.—to meet on a regular basis (usually in return for a nice gift or travel) to review the lawyer's plan, learn about progress and critique future action. It's a powerful motivator set up specifically to encourage emotional (and other) investment in your success.

Make it fun (even silly). As childish as it may sound, writing your week's goals on a whiteboard in your office and illustrating them with hand-drawn or cut-out animals could be just the thing that keeps you going. Different things motivate different people. This could be your hot button—remember doing your chores in return for a sticker on the refrigerator chart when you were 8 years old? Tie into some established psychological pattern that makes you smile!

Get and keep in touch with why you're doing this. Why are you doing this, anyway? If the point of all this is to achieve the career you dream of ... then really dream of it! Set aside some quiet free time to picture what it will be like when you accomplish it. What will you see? What will it smell like? What will you hear? Who will be working with you? Create a complete sensory image in your mind and, when things get crazy, head to that happy place to remember what it is all for. Then return to your marketing efforts.

CHAPTER

24

Steer Clear of These Potholes

As you press forward to mold your practice into your dream occupation, the road will be littered with the wreckage of others who went before you and carelessly fell into unmarked potholes. There will be some unique ones in your path, but let me point out the classics.

Thinking you are too busy to market.
You're smarter than that! The most important time to keep your eye on the marketing ball is when you are really quite busy with legal work. Otherwise, when you stop being busy, you won't have any client work to do and it will take valuable time to crank up the machine again, leaving your revenues in peril. Avoid fits and starts in marketing and make it part of your normal routine.

GETTING IT DONE **139**

> **❝ Don't make the mistake of thinking of selling as making people pay money for stuff they don't want. Selling, the kind you will do, is the act of helping people find solutions to their problems."**

Believing those "all you've gotta do is" stories. If there was a little pink pill you could swallow each morning that would result in new clients beating down your door, there would be no need for all the talking, teaching and whining we do about how to get new clients, right? So, yes, you really do need to make the entire process of business development an integral part of your work as a lawyer. And, no, those other guys didn't do it any "easy way."

Being impatient. Don't be one of those lawyers who says, "I gave a talk at the chamber of commerce last week and I didn't get any clients! This stuff doesn't work." Believe me, it works, but it only works as part of a long-term, integrated effort. Put your head down and work the plan. There is no quick fix.

Refusing to sell. Many lawyers went to law school to avoid ever having to be a salesperson. That may have worked way back when, but it won't work now. In order to do the kind of work you want to do, you have to convince people that you are the one they want handling their matters. Don't make the mistake of thinking of selling as making people pay money for stuff they don't want. Selling, the kind you will do, is the act of helping people find solutions to their problems.

Thinking it is all about you. You've read those lawyer biographies online that shout "I DID THIS!" "I HAVE FANCY CREDENTIALS!" "I'M THE BEST THERE IS!" Yeah, don't do that. Because—and I hate to break this to you—no one really cares about you. The people who are going to hire you to help them only care about their own problem and whether you might have the solution to it. And the only way you can figure out what their problem is and whether you have the solution is by asking about them and then listening.

Mistaking bar association socials for big marketing opportunities. Some bar association events actually can help you build your reputation and thereby attract new clients. (Particularly the events that focus on an area of law that is related to your area of focus—lawyers do refer to others.) But, for the most part, spending all your business development energy and funds hanging out with other lawyers just isn't a great marketing idea. Go find out where the people you want to hire you hang out and be there with them.

Falling for "Sooper-Dooper-Whizbang Lawyer" status. There are businesses that have made a fortune off lawyers by convincing them they have been designated as some sort of king or queen of an area of law and then selling them advertising to promote themselves. Think very carefully before falling for this or any other scam playing off lawyers' need for easy clients. There are a lot of them out there.

- Smile.
- Focus on solving client problems.
- Remember your mission statement. (Read it again!)
- Take care of yourself!

Don't Forget

Here's a reminder of things to keep in mind while working to get clients.

- **Take care of yourself.** If you work too hard, eat poorly, forget to exercise or neglect your rest, your energy and creativity will lag and your lack of enthusiasm will be obvious to all. No one wants to hire a tired lawyer.

- **Focus on solving client problems.** When you shift into getting-clients gear, it's way too easy to fall into *telling* about yourself rather than *learning* about them. Focus, in all you do, on helping clients and potential clients solve problems, get answers to tough questions and resolve conflict. It's all about that client.

- **Remember what you're up to.** You wrote your mission statement at the beginning of this book for a reason. Reread it often and work to keep it relevant.

- **Smile.** I know, it sounds a little bit like something your mom would say. Well, she would say it for a reason. We all just generally like people better who appear to like us. And a smile on someone's face is an indicator of that. People want to hire lawyers who make working together pleasant. So smile.

- **Don't forget, this is a business.** You're not just practicing.